MODELS OF PSYCHOPATHOLOGY

Core Concepts in Therapy

Series editor: Michael Jacobs

Over the last ten years a significant shift has taken place in the relations between representatives of different schools of therapy. Instead of the competitive and often hostile reactions we once expected from each other, therapists from different points of the spectrum of approaches are much more interested in where they overlap and where they differ. There is a new sense of openness to cross-orientation learning.

The Core Concepts in Therapy series compares and contrasts the use of similar terms across a range of therapeutic models, and seeks to identify where different terms appear to denote similar concepts. Each book is authored by two therapists, each one from a distinctly different orientation; and where possible each one from a different continent, so that an international dimension becomes a feature of this network of ideas.

Each of these short volumes examines a key concept in psychological therapy, setting out comparative positions in a spirit of free and critical enquiry, but without the need to prove one model superior to another. The books are fully referenced and point beyond themselves to the wider literature on each topic.

Forthcoming and published titles:

MODELS OF PSYCHOPATHOLOGY

Dilys Davies
and
Dinesh Bhugra

Open University Press

Open University Press
McGraw-Hill Education
McGraw-Hill House
Shoppenhangers Road
Maidenhead
Berkshire
England
SL6 2QL

email: enquiries@openup.co.uk
world wide web: www.openup.co.uk

First published 2004

A catalogue record of this book is available from the British Library

ISBN 0 335 20822 3 (pb)   0 335 20823 1 (hb)

Library of Congress Cataloging-in-Publication Data
CIP data has been applied for

Typeset by RefineCatch Limited, Bungay, Suffolk
Printed in the UK by Bell and Bain Ltd, Glasgow

This book is dedicated with gratitude to Richard and Mike.

Contents

Series editor's preface

A major aspect of intellectual and cultural life in the twentieth century has been the study of psychology – present of course for many centuries in practical form and expression in the wisdom and insight to be found in spirituality, in literature and in the dramatic arts, as well as in arts of healing and guidance, both in the East and West. In parallel with the deepening interest in the inner processes of character and relationships in the novel and theatre in the nineteenth century, psychiatry reformulated its understanding of the human mind, and encouraged, in those brave enough to challenge the myths of mental illness, new methods of exploration of psychological processes.

The twentieth century witnessed, especially in its latter half, an explosion of interest both in theories about personality, psychological development, cognition and behaviour, as well as in the practice of therapy, or perhaps more accurately, the therapies. It also saw, as is not uncommon in any intellectual discipline, battles between theories and therapists of different persuasions, particularly between psychoanalysis and behavioural psychology, and each in turn with humanistic and transpersonal therapies, and also within the major schools themselves. If such arguments are not surprising, and indeed objectively can be seen as healthy – potentially promoting greater precision in research, alternative approaches to apparently intractable problems, and deeper understanding of the wellsprings of human thought, emotion and behaviour – it is nonetheless disturbing that for many decades there was such a degree of sniping and entrenchment of positions from therapists who should have been able to look more closely at their own responses and rivalries. It is as if diplomats had ignored their skills and knowledge and resorted in their dealings with each other to gun slinging.

The psychotherapeutic enterprise has also been an international one. There were a large number of centres of innovation, even at the beginning – Paris, Moscow, Vienna, Berlin, Zurich, London, Boston USA; and soon Edinburgh, Rome, New York, Chicago and California saw the development of different theories and therapeutic practice. Geographical location has added to the richness of the discipline, particularly identifying cultural and social differences, and widening the psychological debate to include, at least in some instances, sociological and political dimensions.

The question has to be asked, given the separate developments due to location, research interests, personal differences, and splits between and within traditions, whether what has sometimes been called 'psycho-babble' is indeed a welter of different languages describing the same phenomena through the particular jargon and theorizing of the various psychotherapeutic schools? Or are there genuine differences, which may lead sometimes to the conclusion that one school has got it right, while another has therefore got it wrong; or that there are 'horses for courses'; or, according to the Dodo principle, that 'all shall have prizes'?

The latter part of the twentieth century saw some rapprochement between the different approaches to the theory and practice of psychotherapy (and counselling), often due to the external pressures towards organizing the profession responsibly and to the high standards demanded of it by health care, by the public and by the state. It is out of this budding rapprochement that there came the motivation for this series, in which a number of key concepts that lie at the heart of the psychotherapies can be compared and contrasted across the board. Some of the terms used in different traditions may prove to represent identical concepts; others may look similar, but in fact highlight quite different emphases, which may or may not prove useful to those who practice from a different perspective; other terms, apparently identical, may prove to mean something completely different in two or more schools of psychotherapy.

In order to carry out this project it seemed essential that as many of the psychotherapeutic traditions as possible should be represented in the authorship of the series; and to promote both this, and the spirit of dialogue between traditions, it seemed also desirable that there should be two authors for each book, each one representing, where practicable, different orientations. It is important that the series should be truly international in its approach and therefore in its authorship; and that miracle of late twentieth-century technology, the Internet, proved to be a productive means of finding authors, as well as a remarkably efficient method of communicating, in the cases of some pairs of authors, half-way across the world.

This series therefore represents, in a new millennium, an extremely exciting development, one which as series editor I have found more and more enthralling as I have eavesdropped on the drafts shuttling back and forth between authors. Here, for the first time, the reader will find all the major concepts of all the principal schools of psychotherapy and counselling (and not a few minor ones) drawn together so that they may be compared, contrasted, and (it is my hope) above all used – used for the ongoing debate between orientations, but more importantly still, used for the benefit of clients and patients who are not at all interested in partisan positions, but in what works, or in what throws light upon their search for healing and understanding.

Michael Jacobs

C H A P T E R   1

Introduction

There are markedly different ways of conceptualizing mental illness in contemporary society, as sociological reviews such as Pilgrim (1997) and Pilgrim and Rogers (1999) indicate. This is reflected in the wide range of terminologies used when referring to psychopathology in academic disciplines and clinical practice. These differing conceptualizations and frameworks for understanding the nature, cause and cure of disturbing experiences are reflected in the various models of psychopathology which we outline in this book.

We begin by overviewing the main models of psychopathology, which can be listed as:

1. The Lay Model;
2. The Legal Model;
3. The Psychiatric Model;
4. Psychological Models: Psychoanalytic, Behavioural, Cognitive, Cognitive-Behavioural, Humanistic, and Socio-cultural; and
5. Sociological Models: Social causation, Social constructivism (labelling theory), and Critical Theory.

Such a wide range of views highlights the controversy surrounding the field of mental illness. As von Bertalanffy writes: 'All scientific constructs are models representing certain aspects or perspectives of reality. This even applies to theoretical physics: far from being a metaphysical presentation of ultimate reality (as the materialism of the past proclaimed and modern positivism implies) it is but one of those models and, as recent developments show, neither exhaustive nor unique' (1987: 62).

Normality and abnormality

Psychology is a wide and eclectic discipline mainly concerned with 'normal' conduct and experience, although concepts of abnormality are considered. Buss (1966) suggests that psychologists have put forward four conceptions of normality/abnormality:

● The statistical concept;
● the concept of an ideal;
● the concept of specific behaviour; and
● the concept of distorted cognitions.

Neither the different models of psychopathology nor the therapies derived from them fall into clear distinct categories, whereby each can be compared readily with the others. Rather there are points of convergence, divergence, and interweaving. This leads to several ambiguities in trying to categorize and clearly delineate concepts of psychopathology. This interweaving can be seen in the following examples.

A. Some models of psychopathology use diagnostic criteria and descriptions based on the psychiatric model. For example, this influence is very clear in the use of psychiatric nosologies within psychoanalysis, as basically the psychoanalytical model uses the same language as the medical model. Clients are often called 'patients' and presenting problems 'symptoms', while 'inner life' is usually called 'psychopathology'.

B. Exploratory therapies, such as psychodynamic and humanistic therapies, in some respects have a similarity with the professional style of both psychiatry and the less exploratory versions of the psychological model, such as cognitive therapy. Although these take an interest in what the patient is saying, they essentially consider this as information with which to build up an expert formulation. The psychiatrist relies wholly on symptoms – what the patient says – in order to make a decision about a diagnosis and to prescribe treatment. The cognitive therapist builds up a picture of the patient's cognitions and a functional understanding of their role in their life. However, when this leads to the person reconstructing some aspect of their life there is clearly a similarity with the therapeutic practices of exploratory psychotherapy. Some have argued (e.g. Bannister 1983) that even a prescriptive behavioural technique such as systematic desensitization is simply one way amongst many in which people come to a subjective reconstruction.

C. Exploratory versions of the psychological model differ from both ordinary conversations and from the prescriptive or structured interviews conducted by many psychiatrists and cognitive-behaviourists. Foucault (1981) discusses the similarities between psychoanalysis and the Catholic confessional. As with the confessional there is disciplinary power – or professional dominance. Although the therapist may control the setting, the patient cannot. The expert retains control of the interpretive framework in the conversation. For example a patient turning up late or not at all is often interpreted as some form of resistance to personal change. The narrative of the client always operates within the therapist's framework and thus, a power asymmetry remains inevitable (Spence 1982). Hayley (1963) discusses the processes of power in clinical psychoanalysis. However, as we shall see when addressing issues related to power later, this issue does not disappear simply because the orientation is Rogerian or any other humanistic therapy.

The lay model

Throughout history and in every culture there is some idea of psychological difference, although what these differences are varies. Even the terms used to describe difference are not identical. However, no culture is indifferent to those who are sad, frightened or unintelligible in their conduct (Horowitz 1983). For example, in Europe from the seventeenth to the twentieth century, such differences were attributed increasingly to medical ideas and less to religious ideas such as demonic possession. Some writers point out that this was the period that madness became 'medicalized' (Scull 1979).

Experts and non experts in the field of mental abnormality recognize madness when they come across it. We come across people whose conduct we find confusing or distressing or frightening to such a point that we call for expert help. If people act in ways that are unintelligible to others they are often dismissed using derisory terms such as 'looney'. When we feel sad or anxious ourselves we might come to a point that we decide to go to the doctor for help. Sometimes this is framed as bad nerves or nervousness although these ideas prefigure concepts of neurosis and psychosis that warrant professional help. More recently the term 'mental distress' has been adopted by service users. However, this does not recognize the often distressing effect on others.

There is a degree of overlap between lay and psychiatric ideas of mental illness. For example, in categories such as anorexia, where there is uncertainty about the cause and the contribution of cultural factors, lay and psychiatric epistemologies are similar (Lees 1997). However, there are also differences between lay and professional perspectives. This is particularly the case with anti-social behaviour. Examples of this may be seen when lay people faced with unacceptable and abhorrent conduct are asked to evaluate the madness or badness in such behaviour. This is evident in murder trials, such as that of Peter Sutcliffe (the Yorkshire Ripper), whose defence was that he was on a mission from God. Jurors dismissed his excuse of mental illness, despite the view of expert witnesses for both defence and prosecution that he was schizophrenic.

There is a mixed lay view about mental abnormality and anti-social conduct. Rosen (1968) points out that in ancient Rome and Athens madness was defined in pre-psychiatric terms by two main features – aimless wandering and violence. A study carried out by Westermeyer and Kroll (1978) in Laos, which at the time had no mental health professionals, explored villagers' perceptions of 'baa' people. These were people who in Western eyes would generally be termed mentally ill. They found that 'baa' people were judged to be violent in 11 per cent of cases before their change of character, but this went up to 54 per cent after 'baa' was identified.

The lay view tends to exaggerate the link between violence and schizophrenia. In the US studies indicate that the public has mixed views about the association of mental disorder and violence. A study carried out by the Feld Institute (1984) showed that 61 per cent agreed with a statement indicating that a person diagnosed as schizophrenic was more likely to commit a violent crime than a normal person. However, another survey (DYG Corporation 1990) found that only 24 per cent thought that mentally ill people were more violent, while 45 per cent of the sample thought that mentally ill people were less violent than others. In Britain studies have also pointed to a mixed lay view of a link between violence and mental disorder which is dependent on a complex relationship between personal experience, beliefs and media messages (Philo et al. 1996).

The legal model

The legal framework is relevant to considerations of psychopathology as it defines the terms and conditions under which mental health professionals can and cannot detain patients and compulsorily treat them.

In the nineteenth century, psychiatry was greatly influenced by eugenics – it was assumed that a variety of deviant conducts could be explained by a tainted gene pool in the lower orders of society. This degeneracy theory, which characterized early biological psychiatry, lumped together the mad, bad and the dim. However, during and after the First World War this framework was challenged. For example, in the forensic field, eugenic ideas of degeneracy, which accounted for criminality in terms of an inherited disposition to bad conduct (Forsythe 1990), were replaced by an increasing interest in environmental or psychological explanations for lawbreaking. Since that time, psychiatric experts have played a major role in identifying and explaining human conduct.

In Britain the law has a definition of mental disorder, which includes four separate conditions: mental illness, mental impairment, severe mental impairment and psychopathic disorder. The first of these is not defined; the second and third refer to those with learning difficulties who are in addition deemed to be dangerous; the fourth refers to anti-social individuals who are 'abnormally aggressive' or who manifest 'serious irresponsible conduct'.

The legal framework leans on psychiatric opinion in two ways. First, because of the absence of precise legal definitions of mental illness, it accepts tautologically that mental illness in a legal sense is the same as psychiatry defines it to be. However, when there is some doubt, the lay view of madness is also taken into consideration by the legal framework. The second way is when certain cases are tried in court, psychiatric opinion is offered as the expert view on the presence or absence of any of the four legal categories. The legal framework accepts that certain forms of badness can be a medical condition. This condition allows offenders the defence of mental disorder and thus absolves them from personal responsibility – although this does not mean that the person will be treated benignly as medically ill. The opposite also holds true – that some are diagnosed as mentally impaired in some way by experts, and legal considerations are given to this view, even if the lay perspective views the person as quite sane and responsible for his/her actions (for example in the case of Ernest Saunders 1990).

As mental illness is not legally defined, judges have sometimes used the lay perspective. For example, in 1974, Judge Lawton commented that the term 'mental illness' involves 'ordinary words of the English language. They have no particular medical significance.' Judge

Lawton referred to the words of Lord Reid in a case when the defendant's mental state was being considered. He commented: 'I ask myself what would the ordinary sensible person have said about the patient's condition in this case if he had been informed of his behaviour? In my judgment such a person would have said "Well the fellow is obviously mentally ill" ' (cited in Jones 1991: 15). This lay conception of legal insanity has been called 'the-man-must-be-mad' test (Hoggett 1990).

Thus in one way the legal framework accepts a psychiatric model, but when this model is found lacking in some respect then the definitions of ordinary lay language are included in the legal framework. This raises issues such as whether madness is for legal and lay purposes a matter of incomprehensible conduct. 'Normal' bad, antisocial or criminal acts are goal directed whereas 'mentally disordered' criminal acts are not directed towards a clear material gain.

In practice, there are two major ambiguities about such a simple legal distinction. First, sex offenders may end up either in prison or in secure psychiatric units, illustrating the confusion in how the legal system judges the motive of sexual gratification. Second, as we have already pointed out, some murderers (for example, Sutcliffe and Neilson) are judged within the lay language of common sense, to be sane, despite the opposite view of expert witnesses. If the legal framework relies on a lay perspective through the jury system to decide the presence or absence of mental abnormality, then the ambivalence we have discussed is likely to be seen in their decisions. Lay people may view on the one hand that a person must be 'sick' or 'mad' to commit dreadful deeds and yet view that such actions deserve the severest of punishments.

Despite the lack of a definition of mental illness in the legal framework, it nevertheless accepts the concept of 'mental disorder'. However, these categories are still open to debate and dispute regarding their basis for diagnosis in specific cases. Also the legal framework delegates the power of identification of mental abnormality to psychiatry, implying acceptance of the psychiatric model. However, the dominant medical considerations at the beginning of the legal process then diminish. For instance, when an abnormal offender is considered for release or 'discharge' from an institution, non-medical people then take part in the decision – lay people and lawyers are members of Mental Health Review Tribunals and take part in the judgements made.

Psychological models

In an overview Buss (1966) outlines three main psychological concepts of normality-abnormality. These are:

1. The statistical concept – for example objective and empirical models, the cognitive-behavioural model;
2. The concept of an ideal – for example the humanistic model;
3. The specific behaviour concept – for example the behavioural model.

The statistical concept

The statistical view holds that frequently occurring behaviours in a population are normal, and thus infrequently occurring behaviours are not normal. This is similar to 'norms' in sociology. For example if we observe the speed at which a person walks – a certain pace would be considered normal. Above this speed, a person might be considered to be anxious, while below it the person might be considered depressed. Most people walk at a rate between the upper and lower limits of this frequency distribution.

However, questions arise, such as who decides on the cut-off points at each end of the distribution and how are such decisions made? Thus frequency of a behaviour in itself does not inform us when a certain behaviour is to be judged abnormal, as value judgements have to be made as to where the cut-off points should be between normality and abnormality. Further, a statistical model may not be valid across cultures – even within the same country. For example, walking slowly may be the norm in a country village, while walking quickly is the norm in a busy city.

In themselves statistical concepts do not inform us why some deviations from the norm are only noted when they are apparent in one direction rather than bi-directional. The example of walking refers to a bi-directional judgement: fast or slow. However, regarding other concepts such as intelligence, negative judgements are only made when outside the norm in one direction. While being 'bright' is valued and will not, without other considerations, lead to being put into the patient role, being 'dim' may well do so.

The statistical approach within the field of abnormal psychology remains influential. Psychologists are taught the parameters of normality and abnormality through the statistical approach, which stresses that characteristics in any population follow a normal distribution. The acceptance of a normal distribution implies that there are underlying assumptions in psychological models of a continuous relationship between the normal and abnormal. However the idea of continuity in one variable does not mean that *ipso facto* there is continuity between other variables. For example, in Eysenck's personality theory (Eysenck 1955), although both neurosis and psychosis follow a normal distribution curve, they are considered to be separate from each other.

The 'ideal' concept of normality

Concepts regarding an ideal for human development are implicit in humanistic and psychoanalytical models. In psychoanalysis, normality is defined when the individual's conscious characteristics dominate over unconscious characteristics (Kubie 1954). In the humanistic model, the ideal person is one who fulfils their human potential or 'self actualizes'. Jahoda (1958) outlines six criteria for positive mental health:

1. Balance of psychic forces;
2. Self-actualization;
3. Resistance to stress;
4. Autonomy;
5. Competence;
6. Perception of reality.

Each of these criteria is problematic. The first two only have meaning within frames of reference that concur with the humanistic and psychoanalytical models. The third, resistance to stress, does not address issues such as its appropriateness. There are some situations where anxiety is normal and adaptive. Further, lack of anxiety under high stress conditions has been one of the defining characteristics of 'primary psychopathy' in the psychiatric model. Similarly, people who tend to avoid human contact, or who are extremely autonomous, may be classified as 'schizoid' or suffering from 'simple schizophrenia'. Competence is a highly variable characteristic, its norms differing according to time and place. Perception of reality has the same problem of inconsistency in definition. For example, in some cultures the ability to see visions and hear voices is esteemed, whereas in other cultures such phenomena would be appraised negatively, and taken as evidence that the person does not share accepted reality.

Specific behaviours

The development of psychology as a scientific academic discipline has been associated with its focus on specific, objective aspects of conduct and on characteristics that are readily amenable to empirical measurement. Academic psychology separated from philosophy, of which it originally formed a part, on the basis of these objective considerations.

The theory of behaviourism tried to restrict the area of concern of psychology to behaviour, and so dismiss subjective experience as unsuitable for scientific enquiry. Although this view no longer dominates psychology, it remains influential. Thus psychologists have tried to operationalize in behavioural terms what is meant by abnormality.

Terms such as 'maladaptive', 'unwanted', 'unacceptable' behaviour are used generally within most psychological models. The advantage of this perspective is that it is explicit in defining abnormality. However, its weakness is that values and norms are left implicit and rarely questioned. The concept of specific behaviour still does not answer questions about who decides what is wanted or acceptable, and what happens when some people find certain behaviours desirable and acceptable and others do not. As we discuss later when considering the socio-cultural model, many theorists point out that it is those holding more influence or power in society who define what is acceptable reality. Hence, what is deemed unwanted or maladaptive behaviour does not have the status of objective fact but rather is socially negotiated. Conceptualizations of psychopathology are relative, reflecting the value system and power relationships of a particular culture at a particular time.

Scientific perspectives

The different models of psychopathology also reflect assumptions regarding the nature of scientific enquiry.

D'Andrade (1986) distinguishes three forms of science: physical, natural and semiotic (systems of meaning). These distinctions are reflected in different academic disciplines:

1. Physical science: for example physics, chemistry, astronomy and related engineering sciences;

2. Natural science: for example biology, geology, oceanography, meteorology, economics, psychology, anthropology and sociology;
3. Semiotic science: for example anthropology, linguistics, psychology and sociology.

Some disciplines such as psychology and sociology occur in both the second and third categories, since there are divergent views about what constitutes legitimate knowledge, and which methods are considered valid to produce such knowledge.

There is an underlying assumption in the first group, physical science, that legitimate knowledge results from studying the lawful relationships that exist in the world. This view of science is characterized by description, explanation and prediction. It also assumes a consensus of empirical description, carried out by independent observers, which is potentially repeatable and falsifiable and so contributes to the production of objective knowledge. Reality is considered to exist independently of its observers. It is also assumed that the findings of scientific knowledge are generalizable from one situation to another.

Most of these assumptions are also found in natural science. However there are two major differences. First, prediction is recognized to be more elusive; nevertheless it is attempted. This is because naturally occurring phenomena such as the life of organisms are open, not closed systems. The second major difference concerns generalizability. Natural events are assumed to be limited to time and place, that is, they are context-specific. However, this group of disciplines still treats the focus of their enquiry as being like a machine that is to be understood. This mechanistic view of the world entails the assumption of determinism, as it attempts to understand causal relationships, and the methodology of this group is concerned with testing hypotheses, and with quantifying or measuring differences between experimental groups or naturally occurring phenomena.

There is a major difference between the underlying assumptions of the above two groups and those underlying semiotic science. In these disciplines, claims to knowledge still involve descriptions, but explanations are considered to be tentative and predictions are almost abandoned. Whereas disciplines in the physical and natural sciences view objectivity as their goal, in semiotic science there is recognition that any understanding of human life entails the understanding of meanings that are imposed or negotiated intersubjectively. Consequently science and its focus of enquiry – that is human life – entails the exploration of meaning. This involves the production and justification of interpretations, but if generalizations are made at all they are made tentatively. Whereas the disciplines in the first two sciences explore causes, in semiotic science the nature of enquiry explores understanding. Its enquiry is not based on hypotheses teasting but upon interpretation, that is it is an inductive rather than a deductive approach.

This conceptual separation of natural from semiotic science was made in the late nineteenth century by Dilthey (1976) who highlighted the differing assumptions underlying the natural and social or cultural sciences. The phenomena to be investigated in cultural sciences require a different methodology from that used in the natural sciences. This idea of understanding in interpretive social science was also highlighted by Max Weber in sociology, and within psychiatry by Karl Jaspers.

In practice, disciplines studying society and human conduct do not neatly fall into semiotic science. For example, psychology uses forms of enquiry that range from physiology to sociology. Thus, as Smart points out, the human sciences cannot be located as belonging in any neat categorization or epistemological arrangement:

> The indeterminate character of the epistemological form of the human sciences leaves a number of methodological and analytical questions and options open. It effectively leaves the human sciences free, or relatively so, to pursue a range of methodological and analytical possibilities, but in addition it means that from the beginning these sciences are in difficulty, are necessarily precarious and uncertain as sciences. (1990: 401)

Smart emphasizes the 'range of methodological and analytical possibilities' for human sciences. In practice such a range has tended to encourage a search for the security of simple answers instead of consideration of the complexities. The search for simple answers can result in reductionism, seen for example in the theory and practice of behaviourism and behaviour therapy.

Social science, such as anthropology, psychology and sociology, spreads across the boundaries of the natural and semiotic sciences. Within each discipline there are differing assumptions about what constitutes science. Thus within social psychology there is both experimental social psychology which is natural science activity, and discourse analysis which is semiotic science activity. Understanding and insights from either of these views of psychology may inform the work of clinicians.

The difference between an approach to science based on

explanation and understanding or interpretation is relevant to the differing views of psychopathology. In this book we refer to these underlying scientific assumptions as they apply to the main models of psychopathology. Our aim is not to reach any firm conclusions about such issues but rather to outline the differing perspectives and conceptualizations of the main models of psychopathology. The whole field of psychopathology is highly debated and there are no absolute criteria that experts can agree on regarding how we view, define and deal with psychopathology. Terms such as mental disorder, mental illness, maladaptive or unacceptable behaviour, or just crazy do not simply have a singly discrete entity to which they all refer.

Although when exploring the various models, there are differences in terminology, there are also fundamental conceptual differences between the models. Each reflects one perception of reality and ignores other aspects. In this way they might be viewed as a fragmented set of perspectives, divided internally and between each other, although at times partly overlapping, with any attempt at integration reflecting yet another model. However, all the models and perspectives on psychopathology that we consider in this book share one characteristic. None of them has been able to conceptualize psychopathology in a way that is universally constant and invariable.

Developmental aspects

During the process of socialization the child learns how to become an accepted member of society. Part of this process involves learning social norms and acquiring the appropriate ways of controlling and expressing emotion. Both these factors are relevant because the field of mental health implicates distressed experiences and distressing conduct on the one hand and deviance from norms on the other.

Freudianism has influenced a variety of social theories. Psychoanalysis offers a theory that links the individual's inner life to the external social context. It provides an account of the emotional life of individuals while at the same time offering an explanation of how mental ill health is determined by society (Jacoby 1975; Holland 1978; Craib 1989).

For Freud, civilization puts limits on the free expression and experience of emotions, especially the instincts of sexual desire and murderous aggression. These limits lead to the need in the child to repress anti-social feeling and behaviour in exchange for family and societal acceptance. The battle between emotions and social conformity leads to the development of neurosis. However, Freudianism provides a partial social theory, since Freud's emphasis is on civilization (Freud 1930) leading to repression and neurosis. Accordingly, we are all to some extent neurotic for more or less the same reasons, balancing our instinctual needs with the constraints of reality. Differences between social groups are thus not addressed systematically by Freud's theory, although later analytically-oriented writers have explored women's issues (Mitchell 1974; Eichenbaum and Orbach 1982). Freud offers an explanation for neurotic behaviour arising from anxiety. Later psychoanalysts have also tried to address other issues such as depression (Bowlby 1969/1982, 1973, 1980) and psychosis (Winnicott 1958, 1965; and Laing 1960, 1966, 1967), by looking at the impact of poor care and separation on the infant (from birth to two years). However, as an example of the divergent views within psychoanalysis, the influential work of Melanie Klein (1932) is distinctive because it focuses more on the pathogenic impact of the infant's inborn aggression rather than the quality of nurturing. Whereas Klein attributes mental ill health as due to instinctual tendencies, Bowlby, Winnicott and Laing are environmentally oriented, emphasizing parental influences, especially that of the mother or primary care giver.

Thus various psychoanalytical accounts consider a general social context ('civilization') to emotional development, and the nuclear family then becomes its main frame of sociological reference. Mainstream psychoanalysis tends to play down or ignore variables other than the family, such as the particular stresses associated with class, race and gender. It also ignores the potentially powerful role of extrafamilial social institutions, such as the school, in shaping the child's identity and emotional life. The psychoanalysts who have looked into these wider areas of theorizing have tended to leave or be rejected by their own professional culture (Reich 1942; Laing 1967; Masson 1990). Psychoanalysis also assumes family relationships that are triangular, or oedipal, that is based on a set of tensions which engender anxiety, created by children relating to a mother and a father. However, in many modern complex societies, children grow up in different family constellations, for example with single or homosexual parents (Miller and Rose 1988).

There is a consensus across many theoretical positions in both sociology and psychology that childhood is a special part of the lifespan. Through the process of socialization, children learn to behave in socially appropriate ways and acquire a confident sense of identity. It is a time when most of the rules and mores associated with the specific socio-cultural context of a child are learned. It is also a time when gender specific conduct is acquired. The child learns what is expected of him/her both at their current age and in the future, through their exposure to adult models of conduct. They learn gradually to control their body and their emotions in order to perform competently and efficiently in the presence of others. The strong emotional expressions tolerated in childhood become less and less acceptable as the person matures into adulthood. Consequently if an adult becomes more exuberant or sad than is deemed appropriate for the context by others, they may acquire the label of 'manic-depressive' (Dreitzel 1973). Children learn the importance of a shared view of reality with their fellows in gaining security and in meriting credibility. All these learned capacities and adherence to societal norms and rules are also bound up with an increasingly elaborate and defined sense of identity. By young adulthood those acting incompetently, immorally or irrationally will be designated by others to be either bad or sick or mad.

Generally, mental illness can be understood as a particular form of difference or 'deviancy' that is not characterized by malice aforethought or motivated by personal gain or gratification, as is the case in criminal behaviour. Part of our expectation of normality is that people will be competent in their social role and their actions intelligible to others. Thus if a person is so fearful or sad that their competence breaks down or acts in ways that we do not understand, such as talking to voices that no one else can hear, we may account for this in terms of mental ill health. Thus mental illness might be understood from a social perspective as failed or incomplete socialization. This perspective is reinforced by the emphasis given by different psychological models on the effect of childhood experience on later life. Most psychologists and psychiatrists assume that problems in childhood make the person susceptible to later mental health problems. Likewise, sociological models of depression in adulthood emphasize developmental vulnerability factors as well as current stressors (Brown and Harris 1978).

These are important issues that need to be considered in all the different psychological models of psychopathology. We begin by describing the psychiatric and biological models. We then consider different psychoanalytical models, before outlining the behavioural and cognitive behavioural models, where psychopathology assumes an equally important place, even if explanations of mental health and illness are different. From there we move to that set of models known as humanistic, where it may appear that psychopathology is eschewed as not fitting the view of the person as self-actualizing. Finally we describe sociological and socio-cultural viewpoints, that psychopathology is as much about society's views as it is about any fine scientific distinctions.

CHAPTER 2

Psychiatric and bio-medical models

Much of psychiatry views psychopathology as being determined by biological processes. The causes of psychopathology are viewed as being some defect that can be cured by some sort of physical/biological intervention. This has been the most widely available and influential of all the models of psychopathology in the western hemisphere, evident in its influence on the structure and content of most other models. For example, cognitive-behavioural and psychoanalytical models use diagnostic criteria and descriptions derived from psychiatry. The use of psychiatric nosologies within psychoanalysis, and its language often draws on the medical: 'patients', 'symptoms', even 'psychopathology'.

The bio-medical model is concerned with the relationship between psychopathology and physiological processes. It suggests that psychological problems are associated with the physical make-up or the chemistry of the brain, physical illness and biological abnormalities of one sort or another. People's behaviour and experience may change if there are physical or chemical changes in the brain or nervous system. Abnormal mental states may be observed from the conduct and experience of those affected by brain injury, drugs, toxins, and fever, while everyday experience shows that behaviour can be greatly affected by biochemistry, for example after the use of alcohol. Many research studies show links between various behaviour patterns and aspects of brain chemistry (Heston 1992). Neurological evidence regarding mental illness indicates that certain bacteria and viruses are associated with manifestations of mental illness as a consequence of syphilis and encephalitis. People with temporal lobe epilepsy may exhibit symptoms from anxiety to florid psychotic states.

These conditions illustrate how mental illness and biological factors are related, and there is broad agreement that *some* psychological problems are caused by physiological or biological factors. However, central to the biomedical model is the more controversial premise that a wide range of psychological problems are caused by biological disturbances and the assumption that psychological problems indicate that something has gone wrong with the normal biological processes. Much of modern psychiatry adopts this perspective. Further, the biomedical model proposes that if some forms of human conduct are related to certain aspects of brain chemistry, then it might be possible to change or control these through chemical intervention.

The historical perspective

The underlying premises of the bio-medical approach may be seen in accounts dating back to ancient Greece and Rome. Sedgwick (1982) describes two broad responses to emotional problems in ancient Rome. One response focused on the body, for example, immersing people who were emotionally distressed in water or drilling holes in their skulls to allow evil spirits to escape. A second approach emphasized good counsel. These two broad views form consistent historical themes, one somatic and the other conversational, the modern-day equivalents of biological psychiatry and the psychological therapies respectively.

The Greek physician Hippocrates (4 BC) believed that psychopathology resulted from bodily disturbances, various forms of 'madness' resulting from different disturbances in the brain. The brain's healthy functioning was dependent on a balance of four bodily fluids or humours, blood, black bile, yellow bile, and phlegm, corresponding to the basic elements of earth, air, fire and water, which must be in a state of balance within the universe. Too much blood led to moodiness, too much black bile to melancholia, too much yellow bile to anxiety and too much phlegm to sluggishness. Such views persisted into the nineteenth century when treatments for physical and mental illnesses included efforts to restore the balance of the humours by blood letting, abstinence from sexual activity and immersion in cold water (Starr 1982).

Before the establishment and dominance of more recent versions of the bio-medical model, people held beliefs about supernatural causes of psychopathology, such as demonological possession and witchcraft. It was in the late eighteenth century and early nineteenth century that the bio-medical model argued that psychopathology was not the result of supernatural forces but of physical illness. At the beginning of the twentieth century, psychiatrists had a narrow remit to deal with lunatics in asylums. These patients were assumed to have disordered brains and were treated accordingly by the limited and crude physical treatments available. By the 1930s psychotic inpatients were treated only with paraldehyde, chloral hydrate, laxatives and cold baths (Bean 1980).

There was very little interest in psychological treatments or in non-psychotic disorders, until the First World War created a crisis for the dominant bio-determinist model of psychiatry. This was built on the assumption that lunacy, along with other forms of deviance such as criminality and idiocy, was the result of a tainted or weak gene pool. This emphasis on heredity was consistent with the prevailing eugenic model. With the First World War both officers and enlisted men began to break down when facing conditions of unimaginable terror. Their symptoms were labelled 'shellshock', later 'battle neurosis' and then 'post-traumatic stress disorder'. Officers were breaking down at a higher rate than lower ranks, and it was inconceivable that they could be labelled as genetically inferior. This crisis of legitimacy for the hereditary model allowed different views of mental disorder, the psychological talking therapies, mainly based on psychoanalysis. Thus by the end of the war, western psychiatry developed into an eclectic discipline encompassing bio-medical and conversational approaches, although a pattern was distinguishable of the neuroses being treated psychologically and psychoses by physical treatments. The latter began to predominate again in the inter-war years with the development of insulin coma therapy (ICT) in 1934, prefrontal leucotomy in 1935 and electroconvulsive therapy (ECT) in 1938.

After the Second World War, mainstream psychiatry marginalized the aetiological role of psychological factors and with it the talking treatment. The main textbooks of the period that dominated post-war psychiatric training reasserted Victorian bio-determinism (Mayer-Gross et al. 1954). Once major tranquillizers were introduced in the mid-1950s, psychiatrists claimed that this breakthrough in treatment enabled patients to be cared for in the community. These historical themes are reflected in contemporary psychiatry. People becoming psychiatric patients may be prescribed physical intervention such as drugs or ECT or some version of psychological treatments or a combination of the two with the former typically predominating. Contemporary psychiatry is a speciality within medicine involving diagnosis, prognosis, aetiology and the prescription of a response to cure or ameliorate the symptoms or condition. This perspective emphasizes illness as being the main explanatory framework for the understanding of variations in conduct troublesome either to the individual (patient) or to others affected by the person's conduct. Psychiatrists who have totally or partly rejected the illness framework have incorporated or adopted alternative views of mental distress derived from other disciplines such as psychology or sociology. Contemporary psychiatry is now generally viewed as being an eclectic discipline (Baruch and Treacher 1978; Ramon 1985; Busfield 1986). However, although social and psychological aetiological factors have been incorporated, biological causes are still viewed as of central importance (Royal College of Psychiatrists 1973), thus distinguishing the psychiatric model from other models of psychopathology. A revision of the model by Clare (1976) gives these other factors equal consideration. It may be argued that such revisions legitimize the disease model in the diagnosis and treatment of people with personal and social problems.

Psychiatric classification

The bio-medical model emphasizes the use of classification. Contemporary classification systems may be dated to the work of Kraepelin, in the late nineteenth century, the most frequently used being The Diagnostic and Statistical Manual of Mental Disorders: Fourth Edition (DSM-IV), published by the American Psychiatric Association, Washington D.C., (1994) and the International Classification of Diseases, Tenth Edition (ICD) published by the World Health Organisation (WHO, 1992). These two systems are similar and most of the comments regarding the DSM system are applicable to the ICD system.

The DSM is considered to be the standard classification of mental disorders. The American Psychiatric Association first introduced DSM-I in 1952 followed by revised editions. It is widely used in psychiatric research as well as for collecting public health statistics. It lists mental disorders that are officially considered part of the DSM system, although most recent editions, unlike the older versions, have not attempted to relate psychiatric disorders to supposed causes. Most disorders are now defined in terms of observable signs and symptoms.

The DSM consists of three major components – diagnostic classification, diagnostic criteria sets and the descriptive text. A DSM diagnosis consists of selecting those disorders from the classification that best reflect the signs and symptoms shown by the individual. For each disorder there is a set of diagnostic criteria, indicating what symptoms must be present (and for how long) in order to qualify for a diagnosis (called inclusion criteria) as well as those symptoms that must not be present (called exclusion criteria). The third component is the descriptive text that accompanies each disorder. The text of DSM-IV systematically describes each disorder under the headings 'Diagnostic Features'; 'Specific Culture, Age, and Gender Features'; 'Prevalence'; 'Course'; 'Familial Pattern'; and 'Differential Diagnosis'. Advocates of this system point out that the use of diagnostic criteria has been shown to increase diagnostic reliability (that is likelihood that different users will assign the same diagnosis).

DSM-IV groups mental disorders along a diagnostic system of five axes or areas of functioning: Axis I lists clinical syndromes; Axis II lifelong, maladaptive personality patterns; Axis III medical conditions; Axis IV psychosocial and environmental problems; and Axis V a global assessment of functioning on a 100-point scale from persistent violence, suicidal behaviour or inability to maintain personal hygiene at one end to symptom free, superior functioning across a wide range of activities at the other.

Disorders classified under Axis 1 consist of the majority of disorders described in the DSM-IV. A summary of the disorders classified are listed in Table 2.1.

Table 2.1 Adapted summary of DSM-IV disorders

Axis 1
1. Disorders usually first diagnosed in infancy, childhood, or adolescence. For example, conduct disorder and infantile autism.

2. Delirium, dementia, amnesic and other cognitive disorders
Problems associated with impairment of brain by injury or illness.

3. Substance-related Disorders
These disorders are identified by substance, for example alcohol, and are conditions in which there is psychological distress or physical damage.

4. Schizophrenia and other Psychotic Disorders
This group comprises most disturbances of thought or cognitive processes including:
Schizophrenia [Paranoid, Catatonic, Disorganized Residual or Unspecified]
Schizoaffective Disorder [Bipolar or Depressive]
Schizophreniform Disorder – similar symptoms to schizophrenia, but duration less than six months.
Delusional Disorder [Grandiose, Persecutory or Mixed]
Brief Psychotic Disorder [with or without marked Stressors, with Postpartum Onset]
Shared Psychotic Disorder [Grandiose, Persecutory or Mixed].

Table 2.1 continued

---

5. Mood Disorders
This group comprises most disturbances of mood including:
Bipolar I Disorder [Manic, Hypomanic, Depressed, Mixed or Unspecified]
Bipolar II Disorder [Hypomanic, Depressed]
Cyclothymic Disorder [rapidly cycling episodes of mood swings with short duration]
Major Depressive Disorder [single or recurrent episode]
Dysthymic Disorder – Chronic minor ('neurotic') form of depression
Mood Disorder due to medical condition, or substance induced.

6. Anxiety Disorders
This group consists of feelings of excessive anxiety or fear including:
Panic Disorder [with or without Agoraphobia]
Agoraphobia [without history of panic attacks]
Specific Phobia [Animal, Natural Environment, Blood-Injection-Injury etc.]
Social Phobia
Obsessive-Compulsive Disorder not to be confused with OC Personality Disorder
Post-traumatic Stress Disorder prolonged reactions (flashbacks, nightmares, agitation, anger, etc.) to experienced trauma
Acute Stress Disorder – immediate (less than six months after the event) reactions to trauma or stressors
Generalized Anxiety Disorder (GAD) – non-specific anxiety
Adjustment Disorder Reactions to changes in the environment, employment, social status, etc.
Anxiety Disorder due to medical condition or substance induced.

7. Somatoform Disorders
This group describes physical symptoms that are not explained by medical issues that cause distress. For example:
Conversion Disorder (converting emotional problems into physical symptoms), Hypochondriasis (excessive and unjustified concern about being sick).

8. Factitious Disorders
Physical or psychological problems that are deliberately produced or faked.

9. Dissociative Disorders
Problems concerning a splitting of consciousness, memory, e.g. multiple personality disorder.

10. Impulse Control Disorders
Inability to refrain from harmful behaviours, e.g. compulsive gambling, pyromania, kleptomania.

11. Sexual and Gender Identity Disorders
Problems involving sexuality, ability to perform sexually, inappropriate sexual orientation, cross-gender identification.

12. Eating Disorders
Problems involving unusual patterns of food consumption, e.g. anorexia nervosa, bulimia nervosa.

Table 2.1 continued

13. Sleep Disorders
Problems in which normal pattern of sleep is interrupted.
14. Adjustment Disorders
Problems in which there is a maladaptive and excessive response to an identifiable stressor.

Table 2.2 illustrates the detail found in most categories in DSM-IV.

Table 2.2 Diagnostic Criteria of Generalized Anxiety Disorder in DSM-IV

This is defined as: Excessive anxiety and worry (apprehensive expectation), occurring more days than not for at least six months, about a number of events or activities (such as work or school performance).
The person finds it difficult to control the worry.
The anxiety and worry are associated with three (or more) of the following six symptoms (with at least some symptoms present for more days than not for the past six months).
Note: Only one item is required in children.

1 restlessness or feeling keyed up or on edge
2. being easily fatigued
3. difficulty concentrating or mind going blank
4. irritability
5. muscle tension
6. sleep disturbance (difficulty falling or staying asleep, or restless unsatisfying sleep)

The focus of the anxiety and worry is not confined to features of an Axis I disorder, e.g. the anxiety or worry is not about having a Panic Attack (as in Panic Disorder), being embarrassed in public (as in Social Phobia), being contaminated (as in Obsessive-Compulsive Disorder), being away from home or close relatives (as in Separation Anxiety Disorder), gaining weight (as in Anorexia Nervosa), having multiple physical complaints (as in Somatization Disorder), or having a serious illness (as in Hypochondriasis), and the anxiety and worry do not occur exclusively during Post-traumatic Stress Disorder.

The anxiety, worry, or physical symptoms cause clinically significant distress or impairment in social, occupational, or other important areas of functioning. The disturbance is not due to the direct physiological effects of a substance (e.g. a drug of abuse, a medication) or a general medical condition (e.g. hyperthyroidism) and does not occur exclusively during a Mood Disorder, a Psychotic Disorder, or a Pervasive Developmental Disorder.

Some disorders have similar or even the same symptoms. The clinician, therefore, in the diagnostic attempt has to differentiate against the following disorders as in Table 2.3, which he or she needs to rule out to establish a precise diagnosis.

There have been many criticisms of the scientific method and of psychiatric classification, with specific criticisms about the DSM system. DSM-IV has attempted to achieve greater reliability by focusing as much as possible on observable behaviours. However, critics point out that subjective factors are involved in clinical evaluation and thus objectivity is questioned. For instance, in Table 2.1, it is unclear what level of anxiety and worry is considered excessive, to fit the diagnostic criteria for generalized anxiety disorder.

Classification systems such as DSM are not static entities but develop over time as knowledge changes. The aim is to describe discrete categories of psychological disturbance. However, as Table 2.3 shows, it is often unclear where one category ends and another begins, and where the boundaries between different disorders should be drawn. This points to possibilities of unreliability in the process of diagnosis. Research concerning the reliability of the diagnostic system indicates that agreement between psychiatrists for some disorders is less than 50 per cent (Zigler and Phillips 1961; Williams et al. 1992). The validity of the diagnostic system, or the extent to which the diagnostic category measures what it was designed to measure, has also been questioned.

Table 2.3 Differential diagnosis

Anxiety Disorder Due to a General
    Medical Condition;
Substance-Induced Anxiety Disorder;
Panic Disorder;
Social Phobia;
Obsessive-Compulsive Disorder;
Anorexia Nervosa;
Hypochondriasis;
Somatization Disorder;
Separation Anxiety Disorder;
Obsessional Thoughts;
Post-traumatic Stress Disorder;
Adjustment Disorder;
Mood Disorders;
Psychotic Disorders;
Nonpathological Anxiety.

A difficulty of the current systems is that they are categorical – someone either has or has not a particular disorder. Categorical systems were criticized by Eysenck (1986) who viewed psychological functioning as a continuum, ranging from one extreme to another. The bio-medical model is based on the idea of a dichotomous split between 'normality' and 'abnormality'. This is the same reasoning as found in categorizations of physical illness, underlining the assumptions of the psychiatric model that mental disorders are an illness.

Biological factors

A great deal of psychiatric research has been carried out to try and determine the influence of biochemical imbalances and genetic influences on psychopathology, and on treatments based on these findings. A central premise is that biochemical imbalances in the brain result in abnormal behaviour. The nerve cells or neurons in the brain form an intricate network and communicate through electrical impulses. These are transmitted through chemicals called neurotransmitter substances. Too much or little of a neurotransmitter substance, or some interference in the neurotransmitter substance between neurons, will interfere with the normal processes for which these neurotransmitters are responsible. For example some research findings suggest that people who are severely depressed often have low levels of monoamines called serotonin and norepinephrine (Coppen and Doogan 1988; Korpi et al. 1986). However, as causality cannot be deduced from correlative evidence, psychological problems may just as possibly cause biochemical imbalances.

Other researchers have investigated genetic defects. It is well established that genes determine physical characteristics such as eye colour. Also developmental genetics indicates that abnormalities in the structure or number of chromosomes are associated with malformations such as Down syndrome. Even though a great deal of research effort has been invested in trying to locate faulty genes, only a few conditions have been specifically identified with them, for example, Huntington's disease. Other disorders that research suggests may have a biological basis include Parkinson's disease, multiple sclerosis, Alzheimer's disease, multi-infarct dementia, brain injury, Tourette's syndrome, AIDS dementia and Korsakoff's syndrome. Some studies suggest a gene for schizophrenia (Bassett et al. 1988), although others have not been able to confirm this finding (Owen et al. 1990). The relationship between genes and behaviour is not direct and is also dependent on environmental factors. This is illustrated by the long-standing nature–nurture debate. Much work has been undertaken highlighting the complex interaction between hereditary/genetic and environmental/social factors in human development. Generally, the bio-medical model has proved useful in investigating organic disorders, and while there is some evidence that biological factors are associated with a range of psychological problems, the direction of causality remains uncertain.

A great deal of psychiatric research has focused on finding biological causes for particular disorders such as schizophrenia. Researchers argue that if schizophrenia has a genetic cause then one would expect that twins are both likely to be diagnosed as schizophrenic. Studies such as Gottesman and Shields (1972) and Heston (1970, 1992) carried out on identical and non-identical twins suggest that the closer two individuals are in biological relatedness, the more likely it is that if one has schizophrenia so does the other. However, those who are biologically related often share similar environments. When investigators have tried to control for this by comparing twins brought up together and those brought up apart, they conclude that the high rate of concordance holds (Gottesman 1991). Nevertheless, caution has to be exercised as methodological difficulties in the statistical analysis of concordance rates have been documented (Marshall 1996). Thus, although some evidence suggests that there may be a genetic vulnerability in some people to develop psychiatric disorders, it is not known exactly how genes are involved.

Criticisms of the psychiatric and bio-medical model

Many criticisms have been made of psychiatric classification generally. There are questions about its reliability and validity, that is the extent to which different clinicians can reach agreement about exactly what criteria makes up the disorder and which disorder is afflicting the person. A difficulty with psychiatry in the illness framework, is that it is mostly concerned with symptoms rather than signs. In physical illness the diagnosis can generally be confirmed using physical signs of changes in the body whereas in psychiatry judgements are usually based on a person's communications rather than on signs of mental illness. This is the case in the diagnosis of neurosis and the functional psychoses, and even in organic conditions such as dementia, brain damage is not always detectable post mortem.

Perhaps the best-known critic of the bio-medical model is the psychiatrist Thomas Szasz (1961a). He argues that mental illness is a myth, as only our bodies can be ill in a literal sense while our minds can only be sick metaphorically. Psychological problems are not illnesses in the same way as flu. Bodily illness is related to mental illness only in the same way that a defective television is related to an objectionable programme. When we call the mind 'sick' we mistake the metaphor for fact just as if the television viewer were to send for the TV repairman because he does not like the programme he is watching (Szasz 1974).

Many critics point out that classification is futile and view psychological problems as products of social forces rather than organic in nature. For example Smail writes:

> Psychiatry's obsession with cataloguing the phenomena of distress into diagnostic syndromes of illness is rendered ultimately futile precisely because the supposed victims of such illness are not carriers of clear-cut cultures of disease, but in essence ordinary human beings struggling to cope with a disordered world . . . Psychiatrists seem to hope that if, like Victorian gentleman scholars sorting out butterflies, they refine their descriptions carefully enough, they will identify species of disease which can be treated medically in the same way that, for instance, tuberculosis can. Widespread criticism of this approach, not to mention its evident fruitlessness, has done nothing over the past hundred years to diminish the enthusiasm of those who engage in it. (1996: 49–50)

Another criticism is that the application of traditional methods to understanding psychopathology is influenced by self-serving concerns. Although science may aspire to principles of objectivity, there is no doubt that in practice scientific research may be influenced by a wider political agenda and sometimes be driven by self interest and other human failings rather than a search for truth. This is true of psychiatric and psychological research endeavours generally (Goldfried 2000). Research within the bio-medical model with its associations with the pharmaceutical industry is particularly vulnerable to such criticism. Breggin's book *Toxic Psychiatry* (1993) raises the question of the relationship between the psychiatric profession and the psycho-pharmaceutical industry. Marshall (1995) quotes Mark Twain's comment that when money talks then truth is silenced.

Critics also argue that social and political aims are inherent (if more covert) in the bio-medical approach. Szasz argues that mental illness was a concept invented to control and change people whose behaviour threatens the social order. Albee (1996) writes of how concepts of mental disorder are developed to support rulers of an exploitative society. Szasz also comments: 'Psychiatric diagnoses are stigmatizing labels phrased to resemble medical diagnoses and applied to persons whose behaviour annoys or offends others. Those who suffer from and complain of their own behaviour are usually classified as "neurotic"; those whose behaviour makes others suffer, and about whom others complain, are usually classified as "psychotic"' (1974: 26). Many studies illustrate how diagnosis can lead to labelling and stigmatization and point to difficulties in distinguishing normal from abnormal behaviour (Rosenhan 1973). Such work indicates the uncertainty of diagnosis which can lead to labelling and how the label once given becomes a self-fulfilling prophecy.

An alternative approach

The medical and psychiatric approach to psychopathology is concerned with description and with causes; but there is a third type of scientific activity, which is concerned with interpretation and understanding. The notion of understanding in interpretive social science was highlighted by Max Weber in sociology and within psychiatry by Karl Jaspers.

In basing psychopathology on underlying human behaviour, Jaspers (1959/1997) suggests that psychopathology is a science that helps the clinician understand certain experiences. Of course, psychopathology is limited by virtue of the fact that the observer can only observe what is being shown and can only understand what is being expressed, and then has to take both the observation and their own understanding to try and make sense of 'abnormal' experiences. There are also problems in dealing with the individual's values. The main concern according to Jaspers (1959/1997) remains with pathological phenomena – these cannot be understood without the context of normality, which the society and/or culture will define.

The notions of conscious and unconscious are relevant to our discussion because it is these that allow access to an individual's inner world. Consciousness is the feeling of awareness of experience, or an object and a resulting self-reflection. Jaspers (1959/1997) pronounces that unconsciousness is a derivative of consciousness. The interaction of psychology and philosophy with psychopathology is crucial in understanding the individual's experiences, which are felt to be entirely personal and individual. Individual cases remain the basic source for all that counts as an experience in psychopathology. Case studies provide the foundation for reading and studying the individual's experiences.

The distinction between subjective and objective is helpful. Subjective experiences are the patient's immediate experience, which can only be indirectly grasped by the observer, whereas the objective can be directly demonstrated in the external world. The distinction between the two is further highlighted in Table 2.4, following Jaspers' observations.

Phenomenology is the study of various phenomena seen in a series of experiences presented or identified by the patient. Psychopathology and phenomenology are both part of the therapist–patient interaction in trying to make sense of the inner world of the individual. Psychopathology offers the context, in conjunction with culture, to clarify, systematize and understand, allowing the clinician to use this understanding in reaching a diagnosis that may lead to appropriate interventions. On a theoretical level perhaps one can look at the psychopathology alone, but in clinical practice psychopathology, clinical diagnosis and management overlap.

Table 2.4 Subjective vs. objective experiences (after Jaspers 1959/ 1997)

Objective	Subjective
1. Outward signs	Through the patient's own statements
2. Phenomena can be tested	These remain unstable
3. Everything perceived by senses	Everything comprehended by empathy
4. Rational content of delusions as understood without empathy	Actual events grasped by sympathetic insight
5. Experiences 'observed' generally in external space	Experiences 'experienced' in the subjective/objective space
6. Aimed outwards	Aimed inwards

C H A P T E R   3

Psychoanalytic models

It is beyond the scope of this book to offer a comprehensive review of all the psychoanalytical schools and their derivatives, but a representative selection of the major theories and significant issues regarding psychoanalytic approaches to psychopathology can be described. The psychoanalytical model originally formulated by Freud has been developed and elaborated in a diverse set of theories. This model has strengths and weaknesses. It provides a comprehensive conceptual framework for understanding cause and effect and potentially can explain all aspects of human conduct. There is also a direct relationship between its theory of causality and the therapy it offers. In some ways Freud transformed psychology from an academic discipline rooted in philosophy that observed and described behaviour, to a discipline that explained and interpreted behaviour.

Although tensions between descriptive and interpretive approaches are evident in the psychoanalytical model between its conceptualizations about intrapsychic mechanisms and its emphasis on interpretation of interpersonal events, it provides a rich hermeneutic framework, which has become part of our intellectual heritage in the Western world. The inherent contradiction is highlighted by the fact that Freud's conceptual framework was formulated within a medical discourse, with his followers constructing typologies of psychopathology that are in line with bio-medical psychiatric classification systems.

Conceptual formulations based on mechanisms such as 'dynamic unconscious', 'psychodynamics' and 'mental mechanism' are consistent with the framework of models derived from Newtonian physics. They are also consistent with a medical model concerned with the mechanical and inner psychical workings of the body. Freud believed that eventually mental events would be explained in terms of neural activity, a reductionist view that is emphasized by Wolman (1968).

However, in contrast to this neurological emphasis, the exploration of symbolism and the interpretation of dreams and words within a personal relationship place depth psychologies within a hermeneutic or interpretive framework. These two dimensions – a mechanistic view of explanation and an interpretive view of understanding and exploration – coexist within the psychodynamic model. As a model it has similarities and differences with other models of psychopathology. Like the bio-medical model, the psychodynamic model assumes that psychopathology is caused by factors internal to the individual. Psychoanalysis has remained largely in the medical field due to its original roots and the dominance of medical practitioners within psychoanalysis. It uses bio-medical classification systems and psychiatric terminology such as 'symptoms', 'diagnoses' and 'patients'. Thus although the psychoanalytical model is fundamentally a psychological model emphasizing the internal determinants of human distress, its conceptualization and terminology are based on the framework and language of a medical or psychiatric model. However, unlike the bio-medical model, it emphasizes internal psychological processes rather than biological or external determinants of human distress. For example a behaviourist may explain someone's conduct as being due to 'the habit of blaming others'; the psychoanalyst may describe the same conduct using terms such as 'fixated in the paranoid position'. Likewise, whereas a behaviourist may describe a person's conduct as being the result of his/her having learnt ways of avoiding others, a psychoanalyst may categorize these same set of behaviours as 'schizoid defences'. Although the psychoanalytic and behavioural approach have different views as to the exact nature of psychological determinants of psychopathology they nevertheless describe internal psychological processes rather than biological or external determinants. Another similarity with the other psychological models is that normality and abnormality are viewed as a continuum rather than as distinct entities. To some degree, we are all ill. This is a reflexive theory, meaning that in principle its theoretical understanding can be applied to everybody.

The model also provides a conceptual framework that can bridge the relationship between the individual and society. The interpersonal school particularly elaborates this view. One of the major developments of the psychoanalytical model, object relations theory, accounts for the relationship between inner and outer worlds.

Some contemporary psychoanalysts adhere to Freud's original views, while others have proposed revisions. Other analysts follow approaches of theorists who originally collaborated with Freud, but later differed in significant ways, such as Jung, Adler and Reich. Some analysts have adopted more radical departures from Freud including theories put forward by Melanie Klein and her followers. What is common to all psychoanalytical theories is the emphasis placed on personal history, which defines them as a biographical psychology.

A central premise is that the mind is divided into conscious and unconscious aspects, and much of our conduct governed by unconscious forces. The dynamic conflict between these different aspects of the psyche leads to various manifestations of mental distress or psychopathology. Further, such conflicts are based on relationships with significant others in the first years of life. A second major premise emphasizes how the manifestations of psychopathology are not random but rather have meanings and patterns that are amenable to understanding.

Sigmund Freud (1856–1939)

Freud was influenced by the neurologist Charcot in Paris, and Breuer in Vienna, both of whom researched hypnosis and hysterical illness showing that physical symptoms could be overcome through the verbal expression of feelings and thoughts. Breuer discovered that the patient Anna O. could express strong emotions during an hypnotic trance, and that when she did so her physical symptoms disappeared. The observation that no mental events are accidental but rather have meanings that are governed by the principles of cause and effect, led Freud to apply the principle of causality to the study of personality.

Breuer and Freud emphasized the concept of the unconscious and its influence on behaviour, proposing that hysterical illnesses are caused by psychological conflicts beyond conscious awareness originating in traumatic experiences that are often sexual in nature. Symptoms of hysteria could be ameliorated through being brought to consciousness awareness. These ideas were the foundation of Freud's later work on the nature of the unconscious and the role of early experience. According to Freud there are instinctual elements within the unconscious inaccessible to the conscious mind, together with other material that has been censored or repressed, but which indirectly effect consciousness. As well as producing psychological discomfort, unconscious processes could produce physical symptoms resulting from the conversion of unconscious psychological conflicts. Freud highlighted how people actively resisted remembering traumatic and unpleasant feelings and events. Symptoms were rather exaggerated expressions of processes common to everyone, that could reveal a person's specific stressors. Similar reasoning was applied to other random or irrational events such as the mistakes of everyday life, or dreams. He also observed that people tend to repeat certain events throughout life, however difficult or painful these experiences, and he called this repetition compulsion. A woman who marries an alcoholic may just be unlucky. However, if this woman happens to marry two alcoholics in succession there is a possibility that personal factors play a role. However, the Freudian concept of psychic determinism does not postulate a simple one-to-one relationship of cause and effect in all mental events. For example, a single event may be over-determined, that is, it is the final common path of many forces.

Freud's original formulations were made before 1910 and termed classical theory. This describes how adult personality is formed through various stages of psychosexual development: the oral stage, anal stage, and the phallic phase. When the child is five to six years of age, it enters the latency stage whereupon the child's sexual motivations become less important. This continues until the onset of puberty at about twelve years of age, when the genital stage of development emerges and adult sexuality develops.

Freud viewed the development of personality in terms of these drives. Successful progression through each of these stages results in healthy psychological functioning in adulthood. However, development never takes place entirely to plan, and characteristics of earlier levels persist alongside the new one. Difficulties during the oral stage are associated with oral personality characteristics in adulthood, such as dependency issues or seeking comfort from eating and drinking. The anal character may possess such traits as stubbornness, independence, or concerns with punctuality and cleanliness. These are reactions against a primitive wish for dirt and disorder. The pre-genital phases are seen as having a fundamental influence upon later adult attitudes towards such basic behaviours as giving and taking, defiance or submission, love or hate, meanness or generosity, optimism or pessimism, and interest or indifference about others.

Freud's classical theory of the aetiology of the neuroses emphasized how difficulties at earlier stages are reflected in later life, due to the fixation of libido at different points, through regression to earlier stages. A present-day frustration or difficulty may bring about regression to an earlier developmental stage. According to this view, in each neurosis there is assumed to be a specific point of fixation for example, the hysteric is said to have regressed to the phallic level and the obsessional to the anal level.

Freud's original views were formulated within a biological framework. Psychic energy was thought of as like 'a fluid electric current' which, when blocked, was deflected and flowed into different forms of neurotic symptoms. In hysteria an intolerable idea was associated with a certain amount of excitation which could only find release in some form of bodily expression. In the case of obsessions and phobias the excitation was detached from its original idea and attached to other ideas which Freud described as suited to but not intolerable. Many neuroses were accepted as being due to heredity defects or to unsatisfactory sexual practices involving excitation without relief or satisfaction. For example, abstinence in those used to more frequent satisfaction led to a release of libido that was transformed into anxiety. Freud's original theory of anxiety focused on the energy of the id and on how when an affect was repressed this energy was channelled or converted into anxiety. Before his later reformulation, Freud's account of anxiety was thus purely descriptive and gave no causal explanation or the origin or meaning of anxiety.

During and after the First World War, Freud developed and modified his theory. He recognized that the terrifying dreams of battle-shocked soldiers could not be explained purely in terms of sexual symbolism or wish-fulfilment and that aggression as well as sex might be an important instinct subject to repression and thus liable to lead to neuroses. From 1920, Freud developed a new theoretical framework called structural theory. The main features of this theory include a theory of personality conceptualizing the psyche as divided into the ego, superego and the id together with a new theory of anxiety and intrapsychic conflict in which the recognition of anxiety as a danger signal plays a central role. This theory highlights the central mediating role of the ego, describes a wide range of ego defences and views aggression as an instinctual drive comparable to libido. In 'The Ego and the Id' (1923) Freud outlined his theory of the total personality. Character structure was now seen as resulting from a three-cornered struggle between the external world, the id (operating at the unconscious level) and superego (concerned with social and moral standards introjected from aspects of childhood caregivers), while the ego (located in preconscious and conscious awareness), tries to balance their different demands. The function of the ego is to confront reality through secondary processes and operates on the basis of what Freud called the reality principle.

Psychopathology according to Freud is based on the intrapsychic balance between the three constituents of the mind. Psychological suffering is due to inner conflicts, often dating back to early sexual experience and childhood of which the person is not consciously aware because of various defence mechanisms. Through psychoanalysis a person can become aware of these conflicts, and renegotiate them through the transference. Emotions and behaviours result from the interaction between these three components. The id seeks immediate gratification and operates on the pleasure principle, however, if gratification is not immediate it is sought in with fulfilment through the generation of fantasies of what is desired through what Freud termed primary process thinking.

The primitive impulses of the id are dealt with so as to make them compatible with external reality and the moral strivings of the superego. This is done in several ways so that adult character traits may be the result of either:

- an aim-inhibited or sublimated expression of pregenital libidinal drives, or
- a reaction formation against such drives, or
- a residue of pregenital drives.

Thus the striving for power or any form of self assertion may be seen as an expression of aim-inhibited sadism; any kind of affection as an expression of aim-inhibited sex; and sculpture as a sublimation of anal eroticism. In all these cases the ego has formed a channel rather than a dam for the libido which is directed on the whole along socially approved lines. Sublimations are characterized by the relatively smooth flow of pregenital drives towards alternative goals, and by the choice of goals being acceptable to society. Another mechanism is reaction formation where the forbidden impulse is repressed and appears as its opposite, which then serves both to maintain the repression and present the ego to society favourably.

According to structural theory while both anxiety and fear are reactions in the face of a dangerous situation, fear is a response to a known and external danger, and anxiety to an internal and unknown one. The source of danger in anxiety is instinctual when powerful and forbidden desires threaten to overwhelm the ego and endanger the individual's relations with others. There is a hierarchy of sources of anxiety: loss of the union with the mother at birth, loss of the breast at weaning or of the penis at the phallic stage, loss of approval of the superego or of social and moral approval of significant figures in the latency period, and society in adult life. Separation from the mother is the prototype of all subsequent anxiety up to and including the fear of death. In his second theory of anxiety, Freud suggested that anxiety arises not in the unconscious but in the ego itself: 'We may now take the view that the ego is the real locus of anxiety, and reject the earlier conception that the cathectic energy of the repressed impulse automatically becomes converted into anxiety' (1926/1959).

Freud described how neurotic anxiety and guilt are dealt with through unconscious distortions of reality through the use of various defence mechanisms. Repression is an especially significant defence as it operates to keep unacceptable impulses unconscious. However, as the repressed wish still exists in the unconscious, it may find expression in other ways. This is true of other defences such as denial, projection, reaction formation, displacement, intellectualization, regression, identification, sublimation and rationalization. The defences often betray the repressed indirectly, a phenomenon Freud called 'the return of the repressed'. Thus the reaction formation of compulsive washing, in an attempt to wash clean impure ideations, may in itself give sensuous pleasure, and so displace the forbidden wishes.

According to Freud's fully developed theory there are two basic instincts: a life instinct, or Eros; and a death instinct, or Thanatos. The life instinct comprises the old concept of libido and is a self-preservation drive. The death instinct was a new concept which Freud viewed as being separate from the libido, representing an innate destructiveness and aggression directed primarily against the self. While the life instinct is creative the death instinct is constantly working towards death and ultimately towards a return to the original inorganic state of complete freedom from tension or striving. This theory is outlined in *Beyond the Pleasure Principle* (1920/1955). However, many of Freud's followers disagreed with his view that aggression and the death instinct are synonymous.

Freud viewed inwardly directed aggression from whatever source as dangerous to the individual. There is a constant necessity to deal with it to make it less destructive. This may be done in one of two ways: first by eroticizing it, that is, by combining it with libido taking the form of sadism or masochism (sexual perversions in which sex and aggression are combined); and second by directing it outwards in aggression against others. Suicide is a failure to preserve the self by these means. Many lesser forms of self damage can be attributed to the inwardly directed death instinct, from unconsciously motivated accidents, self-inflicted diseases, addictions and failures, to the more dramatic crimes committed with the unconscious intent of being found out.

Thus the psychoanalytical model originally conceptualized psychopathology as being the result of unconscious forces and later, in the formulation of the mind being divided into three parts, the id, the ego and the superego, as a result of conflicts between different parts of the personality.

Using concepts from classical and structural theory some psychoanalysts began applying the psychoanalytical model to psychosis. Freud himself highlighted two fundamental concepts regarding the psychoses. One was that of narcissism, and the second that of libido economy, that is the distribution of quantities of psychic (libidinal) energies and how they affect mental functioning. Based on the way energy is distributed in the psyche, Freud classified the symptoms of schizophrenia into three categories. According to this model, the process of schizophrenia is due to energy invested on objects in the external world (object libido) being transformed into energy invested on the self (narcissistic libido). Thus, psychotic symptoms are consequences of a massive redistribution of libidinal investment (cathexis) from representation of objects to representations of the self. In schizophrenia the refocusing of energy leads to an essentially narcissistic state characteristic of the very young infant. Because of the similarity with early childhood, many authors have concluded that such regression must have been conditioned by a trauma or series of traumata in the earliest months of life. For this reason, a major aetiological role in schizophrenia was assigned to early parenting such as the 'schizophrenogenic' mother. This has led some theorists to view psychosis as a disturbance specifically experienced during the oral phase.

This classical model of psychoanalysis has had far-reaching implications in the psychoanalytical understanding of the psychoses. Even though the later structural model of Freud tends to be the preferred model for the understanding of the neuroses, theories and ideas generally regarding the impairment of ego functions in schizophrenia have been based on the assumptions of the classical model.

However, many analysts have in addition also applied Freud's later theories of mental functioning – ego psychology, the theory of aggression and the theory of anxiety and defence – to the psychopathology of the psychoses. These contributions mostly take the form of additions, or elaborations of various aspects of Freud's original theory rather than representing a break with Freud's views, but they still adhere to two basic concepts of Freud's early work: first, psychosis is initiated by the withdrawal of investment in objects (decathexis); and second, this first stage of psychosis is generally followed by a restitutive phase (recathexis) characterized by the appearance of delusions and hallucinations.

The later contributions to the psychoanalytical model of the psychopathology of the psychoses are in agreement with Freud's view that the essence of psychoses is a break with reality, and that the explanation for this break is the withdrawal of investment in the mental representations of some or all of the objects of the outer world.

Arlow and Brenner (1969) for example, suggest a framework for a more comprehensive and integrated psychoanalytical understanding of the psychoses in which the clinical data on psychoses can be conceptualized more coherently and consistently. They apply to the psychoses Freud's later views of the formation of symptoms in the neuroses and group psychotic symptoms according to the role they play in intrapsychic conflict. In the psychoses, the ego's defence mechanisms attempt to ward off threats of being overwhelmed by anxiety resulting from some intrapsychic conflict through instigating different kinds of compromises, such as distortions of character, symptom formation and severe inhibition, between the conflicting mental forces. According to classical theory delusions such as the imminent end of the world are due to the patient's awareness of massive redistribution of libidinal investment. However, this does not give adequate consideration to the role of conflicts over aggression and guilt. Melanie Klein and many others have highlighted the significance of conflicts over aggressive impulses in the psychopathology of the psychoses. Arlow and Brenner view that the end of the world delusion can be explained more meaningfully using concepts of conflict and defence from Freud's structural theory. The delusion that the world is coming to an end may represent a defensive projection of destructive wishes directed either towards objects and/ or towards one's self. In this way, superego reproach is avoided. As the cause of the world's predicament is attributed to forces external to the patient, s/he is free of blame. Such an explanation would place world destruction fantasies in a closer relationship with delusions of saving the world. Arlow and Brenner point out that clinical data indicates that such delusions of world destruction and world salvation frequently occur together and are best viewed as two sides of a conflict over guilt-laden aggressive impulses. In Freud's classical view of the psychopathology of the psychoses, these delusions belong to two different phases of the illness and result from two different types of processes. The end of the world delusion is connected with the phase of decathexis; the messianic or saving delusion with the phase of restitution.

A second category of symptoms in classical theory encompasses delusions of grandeur and hypochondriasis. These symptoms are assumed to result from massive withdrawal of energy vested in objects and its transformation into energy vested on the self. In hypochondriasis, the hypercathexis of the body results in the patient's excessive preoccupation with his or her body and its functioning. Thus, hypochondriacal anxiety is viewed as essentially a toxic process resulting from an excessive accumulation of libido. However, this version based on anxiety being transformed libido does not take account of Freud's later views regarding the role of aggression in mental conflict, or the signal function of anxiety. Arlow and Brenner view that hypochondriacal symptoms in the psychoses have meanings related to conflicts and their psychodynamics are identical with the structure of the conversion symptoms of hysterical patients.

Arlow and Brenner point out that although there are significant differences between the neuroses and the psychoses, these reflect variations in the degree of severity. The processes themselves, for example, fixation, trauma, conflict, regression, and so on, are qualitatively the same in both categories of mental illness. The following characteristics distinguish the psychopathology of the psychoses from the neuroses:

1. Regression tends to be more severe and pronounced in the psychoses than in the neuroses. Prephallic fixations and conflicts over derivatives of these drives are particularly prominent. However, this does not preclude the fact that typical phallic conflicts may play an important role in the psychoses.
2. In the psychoses, conflicts over aggressive impulses are more intense and more frequent than in the neuroses. Because of these impulses, the patient has a special need to protect objects from his/her own aggression. As a result, serious disruption in the patient's relationship with people and objects in the external world are likely to be prominent.
3. One of the most important distinguishing features of the psychopathology of the psychoses is that the disturbances of ego and superego functioning are much more severe than in the neuroses. Whether faulty ego and superego functioning in the psychoses is

due to nature, nurture or the consequence of regressive deterioration in the psychoses is a question of debate between psychoanalysts. For example, Hartmann (1950, 1953) has called attention to the importance of studying the genetic factors that may be responsible for the predisposition to regression of ego functions in adult life. Beres (1956), studying deviant children, suggested that certain developmental traumata at specific phases in childhood might lead to psychoses in adulthood.

4. As the ego of the psychotic patient is especially weak (Hartmann 1950) intrapsychic conflicts become overwhelmingly acute and hence the ego resorts to extreme measures of defence. Regression is the main characteristic. Extreme forms of denial, projection, isolation and introjection are also typical of the ego's defensive system in psychosis.

Carl Gustav Jung (1875–1961)

Jung began his career at the Burghoeltzli Mental Hospital in Zurich where he remained until 1909 under Eugene Bleuler, working with hospitalized patients with major mental illnesses, most notably schizophrenia. Based on his work exploring meaning in the words and behaviour of schizophrenic patients, Jung extended the work of Pierre Janet to formulate a theory of the psychoses which he outlined in his classic study in psychopathology *Psychology of Dementia Praecox* (1907). His formulations provide a conceptual link between the neuroses and the psychoses, and his clinical delineation of split-off complexes influenced Bleuler's choice of the term 'schizophrenia' (Bleuler (1911: 476)) which replaced Kraepelin's term 'dementia praecox'.

Early in his career Jung developed a word association test, thus linking experimental psychology with psychoanalysis (*Studies in Word Association* 1914, 1916, 1919). Jung went on to develop his own theories and technique of psychotherapy which is termed analytical psychology.

Despite initially being a disciple and then a colleague of Freud's there are fundamental differences between the two men over the nature of libidinal energy and over infantile sexuality as the cause of neurosis. As early as 1907, Jung disputed whether sexuality was the central factor (1907: 59), and in *Symbols of Transformation* (1912) and *Theory of Psychoanalysis* (1913b) Jung put forward a new concept of libido, purely energetic and desexualized. This was an outright rejection of Freud's view of the libido as exclusively sexual or pleasure orientated in origin and that sexuality alone was the prime motivating force. In Jung's view libidinal energy was only one of several motivating forces. For example he noted that the hunger drive is more appropriately viewed as a survival instinct rather than one devoted to the pursuit of pleasure. Jung hypothesized that libido is non-specific psychic energy and can be channelled. Freud viewed the unconscious as containing unacceptable sexual and pleasure impulses repressed since childhood and located solely in the past, whereas Jung emphasized that libido (or impulses) arising from the unconscious has relevance to both the past and present. Whereas Freud saw the libido as essentially sexual in nature, Jung viewed it as essentially spiritual. Jung also challenged Freud's basic tenet of the Oedipal complex. Although acknowledging that boys become powerfully attached to their mothers, potentially bringing about conflict with their fathers, Jung denied that either attachment or conflict was inevitably sexual. Instead he described the son's attachment for his mother as being spiritual rather than physical or sexual in nature, reflecting a need for psychological renewal.

According to Freud the ego has an intermediary function in the conflict between the id and superego. However, Jung argued that the superego is not separate from the ego. Instead he termed the part of our ego which is concerned with parental and societal values and expectations as the persona – our mask to the outside world. The persona is conscious while the superego is partly unconscious. Jung also conceptualized another part of the unconscious that compels us forward termed the Self. While Jung recognized that the unconscious contained repressed material, he also emphasized its positive side, as the source of psychic energy and creativity pushing us forward to higher levels of consciousness. Jung found Freud's theory of dream interpretation and wish fulfilment too rigid and reductive, ignoring the paradox and ambiguity of unconscious contents.

A major difference with Freud concerns Jung's views of the process of development. For Jung this occurs across the lifespan rather than solely concerned with childhood processes. He introduced the concept of individuation, a process beginning at about forty years of age. This is the inner force or drive, ingrained in the species and present in the individual psyche that compels us towards personal growth and development of the self. An integral component of this process is the individual's drive for meaning. Jung also emphasized the spiritual or religious function of the psyche and thought that its repression could lead to neurotic or psychotic manifestations of psychopathology.

This drive enters our consciousness intermittently, calling for change or, more precisely, the continuation of mental evolution. Jung viewed neuroses not only as a disturbance but also as a necessary impulse to broaden a consciousness that is too narrow, and thus acts as an incentive to maturation and healing. From this positive view, a psychic disturbance is not just a failure, illness or arrested development but a drive towards self-realization and wholeness. Jung also viewed dreams as pointing the way forward and not just concerned with the past. The positive emphasis on growth encouraging interpretations of psychological experience has some links to the humanistic models of psychopathology.

Analytical Psychology

In his *Analytical Psychology*, Jung developed a psychological typology that delineates attitude types (introvert-extrovert) and function types (feeling-thinking, sensation-intuition). Every person can be classified according to one of the four basic function types determining their typical way of experiencing reality. The psyche in Jung's model is an auto-regulated system, combining the typical characteristics formed by influences as species, race, nation, and the spirit of the age with uniquely personal ones. Its functioning results from the interrelation of the two realms of the unconscious (personal and collective) and their relation in turn to consciousness. The ego identifies with the conscious mind acting as a filter so that all ego reflections go to the personal unconscious. The personal unconscious includes both memories easily brought to mind and what Jung described as lost memories, repressed painful idea and subliminal perceptions and content not yet ready for consciousness. These repressed thoughts and feelings form clusters or complexes in the personal unconscious. The third part of the psyche in Jung's theory is the collective unconscious or 'psychic inheritance'. Freud did not see the necessity of such concept which became one of the main reasons for their rift.

Jung viewed that thoughts, feelings, and memories group themselves into dynamic clusters of complexes. Jung's conceptualization of the collective unconscious and the function of archetypes developed from his exploration of his own dreams and from his studies of the dreams, hallucinations and delusions of his schizophrenic patients. He explored delusory systems, comparing them with mythological and cultural themes, which led to his idea of primordial images and later to his ideas on collective (archetypal) material in the unconscious psyche. Complexes are the means by which archetypes manifest themselves in the personal unconscious.

Jung observed that many of the images related to him by patients reflected recurring mythological images and symbols universal to mankind. From these observations he went on to conceptualize the collective unconscious which he describes in 'Man and his Symbols' (1957) as an inaccessible layer of the psyche containing universal experiences and images. He described it as being the reservoir of our experiences as a species, a form of knowledge we are all born with yet not directly conscious of influencing all our emotions, experiences and behaviour. We only know about it indirectly by looking at those influences. Examples of the effects of the collective unconscious include the spiritual experiences of mystics, dreams, fantasies, fairy tales and the immediate recognition of certain symbols and the meanings of certain myths. Jung viewed that all such examples could be understood as the conjunction of our outer reality and the inner reality of the collective unconscious.

Archetypes are the central organizing structure of a complex. They are the innate forms of the psyche consisting of universal primordial images and patterns of symbol formation recurring throughout humankind. They are not inherited images as such but rather inherited possibilities predisposing us to form typical image. Jung viewed that archetypal patterns were biologically determined although their manifestation in imagery often carries a symbolic meaning for the individual. The unconscious aspect of an event is revealed to us in dreams because in dream-like states where consciousness is not present to protect the ego from the manifestations of the unconscious, it appears not as a rational thought but a symbolic image. The four important archetypes that play a very significant role in everyone's personality are the Persona, Anima(us), Shadow and the Self. The archetype of the Self is both the totality of the personality, conscious and unconscious, and the process of becoming of the whole personality. Jung viewed our deepest needs to be for meaning and purpose and saw religious practice as a fundamental archetypal need and deprived of its symbolism, individuals were cut off from meaning, and societies perished. Meaning can be found through dreams and their symbols in the form of archetypical images, arising from the collective unconscious. Jung defined neurosis as the suffering of the soul which has not discovered its meaning.

Psychopathology

It is in the field of schizophrenia where conceptual differences between Freud and Jung are most apparent. Jung elaborated Janet's concepts concerning the neuroses and applied these to the study of schizophrenia (1911). He considered that the primary symptoms of schizophrenia as described by Bleuler (1911) were defensive reactions of the individual due to being 'overwhelmed' by the complexes. A psychotic episode occurs when the unconscious overwhelms the conscious psyche as it effectively shuts out and represses the psyche as a whole. Jung viewed psychopathology as being a continuum, conceptualizing a similarity between diverse psychological states, for example between certain mechanisms underlying the formation of symptoms in hysteria and the symptoms in dementia praecox (1907: 62–83), that is between the neuroses and the psychoses.

Jung considered biological factors as part of the aetiology of schizophrenia including the possibility of an unknown 'brain toxin' as a causal factor. He later elaborated his theory describing a biological or instinctual format of the mind or psychosomatic organizations of complexes. Jung emphasized the role played by the complexes in schizophrenia where they would split completely from conscious control, 'swallowing' completely the ego and producing psychotic symptomatology. Thus, although psychotic visions illustrate an access to the collective unconscious, the person has been in effect consumed by it, resulting in a loss of ability to function and relate. Jung described this split-off quality of the complexes as being physiological and unsystematic, and radically different from their expression in the neuroses (1939/47). Schizophrenic symptoms could not be understood as just a reflection of archetypal imagery:

> This is usually not the case, any more than it is in normal dreams; here as there the associations are unsystematic, abrupt, grotesque, absurd, and correspondingly difficult if not impossible to understand. Not only are the products of schizophrenic compensation archaic, they are further distorted by their chaotic randomness. (1958)

A complete split between the ego and the complexes results in disintegration in the personality as the schizophrenic identifies with unconscious content. Schizophrenic symptoms seem so bizarre because the general symbols manifested by the collective unconscious are so far removed from a particular individual that they may appear as being beyond comprehension. Their oddness brings about an even greater resistance by the conscious psyche resulting in the contents of these manifestations becoming even more distorted and stranger.

Jung also recognized the role of psychological factors in schizophrenia (1919). He pointed to evidence for this in the changes produced in the illness after environmental modifications (the disappearance of a great number of catatonias after the reform of the asylums), in psychological factors precipitating onset and relapse, and above all in the existence of a great number of cases of latent schizophrenia usually hidden behind a neurotic façade, which emerged in the course of psychological treatment. Nevertheless, Jung claimed that psychological factors alone were not enough to explain schizophrenia. He hypothesized a 'special predisposition' or 'abnormal sensibility'. Due to an external conflict or internal imbalance in the psyche the unconscious responds with a complementary attitude trying to re-establish the psychic equilibrium. In normal circumstances this occurs successfully. However, in the psychoses there is an attempt to escape from the unconscious compensatory trends. The precipitating factor may arise from ignoring or defending against unconscious manifestations and refusing to accept its compensatory significance, for example, the content of one's dreams, whose function is to compensate for deficiencies and to warn of present dangers. This consequently reinforces a vicious cycle, as lack of awareness of unconscious manifestations results in an intensification of the unconscious compensatory strivings. Jung described how the resultant split was disastrous because 'the unconscious soon begins to obtrude itself violently upon the conscious processes. Then come odd and incomprehensible thought and moods, and often incipient forms of hallucination, which plainly bear the stamp of the internal conflict' (1914: 63).

Jung viewed the symptoms associated with schizophrenia, which illustrate the collective unconscious, as connected to normal dreaming because the unconscious material is identical in both. Schizophrenics could be described as existing in a dream-like state. He described dreaming as a mental condition in which formerly unconscious elements are given the value of real factors to an extent that they take the place of reality. Elements of the collective unconscious will be most likely to appear when one is relaxed and off guard, such as in dreams and day time fantasies because these things are the least controlled by a conscious sense of the limits of real life and they are more apparent in all cases of serious psychoses. From this perspective, Jung viewed that the dreamer is normally insane.

Thus Jung developed a theory about the psyche, radically different from Freud's. He saw individuation as a developmental process, manifested through adulthood and in symbolic life. He focused his psychotherapy on the development of individuality by means of increasing self-awareness. Jung's rich exploration into the contents of psychoses was a hermeneutic study of huge scope offering an alternative to theories postulating an ontological split in the psychoses. His pioneering work in applying psychodynamic concepts to the psychoses has had great influence in later theoretical developments.

Alfred Adler (1870–1937)

After his break with Freud, Adler went on to develop an individual psychology. Like Jung, he criticized Freud's emphasis on sexuality, and Freud in turn criticized Adler's emphasis on the role of conscious processes and on the social context.

Individual psychology views a central motive of human personality development as a striving for unity of the ego. Through creating goals in life we attain a sense of purpose and then strive to achieve these goals. We create an image of an ideal self that represents the perfect person we strive to become. Inferiority feelings in relation to our perfect self are normal. The drive to overcome the sense of inferiority is the stimulus for our striving towards superiority. For example a child who felt intellectually inferior may as an adult strive to become intellectually superior. Adler also pointed out how the position in one's family – birth order – influences lifestyle. He emphasized the social nature of human beings and how interpersonal relations and the social context into which we are born, shape the personal goals we choose to strive towards.

Adler viewed human behaviour in terms of a struggle for power in order to overcome feelings of mental or physical inferiority. Describing how people strive for control and power over their lives, he highlighted how early childhood experiences of powerlessness can later result in feelings of inferiority. The manner in which an individual deals with such feelings gives rise to a particular psychopathology, for example, by withdrawing or by being abusive and bullying; or families characterized by neglect and abuse may produce children who strive for perfection using pathological selfish goals such as seeking attention or revenge. Adler showed how the desire of realizing fictional goals created early in life influences the present. The goal of therapy is to encourage awareness of thorough consciousness raising facilitated by such means as a lifestyle analysis of factors such as a person's family background, sibling position and how the individual came to his/her personal construction of the world.

Adler's concepts influenced some later psychoanalytical developments, such as the emphasis on neurosis as a disorder of the total personality, that the ego plays a large part in its genesis and that non-sexual factors also lead to conflict. His lifestyle analysis has similarities with the cognitive approach of Ellis and Beck (Ellenberger 1970).

Interpersonal psychoanalysis – the neo-Freudians

Brinich and Shelley suggest a strong connection between the founders of interpersonal psychoanalysis such as Horney, Fromm and Sullivan and the Adlerian school, since the neo-Freudians 'move in the Adlerian direction, towards the social world and its contextual interconnections with the interiority of the psyche' (Brinich and Shelley 2002: 53). Neo-Freudians tend to reject the Freudian view of personality development which emphasises the repression of unacceptable impulses. Rather, they view it as being shaped by early repeated interpersonal experiences with primary objects. Within this broad approach one of most influential writers for the study of psychopathology was Harry Stack Sullivan.

One of the central themes in Sullivan's theory is that everything in our inner world originates with our early interpersonal relationships. It follows that certain family patterns lead to the development of different clinical patterns. Sullivan studied human character and described two 'integrating tendencies'. These were the pursuit of satisfaction and the avoidance of anxiety. In his theory Sullivan outlines the development of the self-system with its characteristic dynamics. The resulting patterns are either successful or unsuccessful, and define the differences between clinical groups. He criticizes the concept of diagnosis, pointing out that diagnostic labels neglect the role of the 'other' in interpersonal interaction. Some later interpersonalists such as Daniel Jones (1997) criticize Sullivan for changing his emphasis from developmental syndromes to more diagnostically based clinical entities (disorders that result from extreme security-seeking dynamisms during periods of stress). Jones cautions against the mistake of construing, for example, Sullivan's use of the label 'obsessional' as being equivalent to the 'static label' used in other models. In the interpersonal model, the significant factor is the *unique* pattern of security seeking and anxiety avoidance of the individual rather than the diagnostic label assigned to them. Like others in the interpersonal model, Sullivan is opposed to rigid theorizing and interpretations based on such theorizing as often found in psychoanalysis where interpretations are based on the assumption that all human motivation rests upon a universal sexual substrate.

In a review of the interpersonal's model perspective on psychopathology Celani (1997) discusses studies applying this approach to interpersonal diagnostic categories. Diagnostic entities in the interpersonal approach are forms of psychological adaptation representing different interpersonal styles developed in relation to an anxiety-provoking environment.

The interpersonal model provides its own understanding of the psychoses, with schizophrenia well represented. Sullivan suggests that the most puzzling and disturbing schizophrenic behaviour can be understood as a reasonable response to actual interpersonal events during the individual's developmental history. Later interpersonal theorists have elaborated on his views: for example, Blechner (1997 cited in Celani 1997) describes the multiple and distorted ways the individual tries to maintain a degree of security in the face of an interpersonal world that has failed him or her.

Interpersonal theorists view the meaning of schizophrenic verbalizations not in terms of content, but as relationship-defining devices. Blechner (1997 cited in Celani 1997) emphasizes the importance of understanding the patient's communication by deciphering the patient's interpersonal goals. Theoretical concepts based on the interpersonal model are applied to paranoia and its clinical treatment in the work of O'Leary and Watson (1997 cited in Celani 1997). They highlight Sullivan's concept of the 'substitutive process', in which the fragile and damaged view of the self is replaced by an inflated and grandiose view, and the extreme nature of paranoid defences. A person's hypersensitivity to humiliation, along with an underlying impoverished sense of self, can over time result in such defences, which cause extensive damage to the self system and once in place are resistant to change.

Contemporary applications of the interpersonal model of psychopathology to the psychoses may be seen in such work as, Blechner (1997); O'Leary and Watson (1997) and Youngerman (1997).

Youngerman who applies the model to the borderline personality – a group not studied much by interpersonal theorists but of central concern in ego psychology and object relations theory. Object relations theorists, notably Fairbairn, define the borderline personality entirely in terms of internalized objects, splitting and the moral defence, concepts avoided by interpersonal theorists. Sullivan criticized views based on assumptions of the existence of internal objects as 'reckless simplification' (1953: 166). Youngerman (1997 cited in Celani 1997) developed a perspective on the borderline disorder that maintains the interpersonal model's positions on nosology, hierarchy, diagnosis-versus-character, and structure-versus-process, using three personifications (the good-me, the bad-me, and the not-me) and the lack of tenderness typical of the histories of borderline patients to account for their rapid interpersonal shifts. The not-me experience is a result of such intense rejecting behaviours that they are not accessible in normal awareness. They appear in a dissociated state suddenly and inexplicably. Sullivan's (1940) account of the 'self-adsorbed' character also describes this dichotomous view of self and others.

The interpersonal approach has been applied to a wide range of categories subsumed under the general heading of the neuroses, for example, anorexia (Bruch, 1973); obsessional disorders (Winckler, 1997); hysteria (Lionell, 1997); addiction (Brisman, 1997). Winckler's (1997) study of obsessive disorders outlines the typical family background of patients with this disorder, featuring the role of mystification, the covert abuse of power by the parents, and the necessity for developing forceful defences against awareness of the intolerably painful realities of childhood.

In a review of the interpersonal perspective on hysteria Lionell (1989) emphasizes the importance of Chodoff and Lyons's (1958) work distinguishing the diagnosis of hysteria from conversion reactions and from inferred internal dynamics. This defines hysteria interpersonally rather than libidinally and has encouraged many interpersonal theorists to explore the disorder. Lionell develops the concepts of 'self-as-agent' and 'self-in-relation' to explain why the hysteric's continual interpersonal success never feeds back to strengthen a sense of self. The hysteric interacts with others defensively in order to reduce anxiety, and hence factors such as interpersonal success, effectiveness or affability, do not enhance or expand self-as-agent. Self-experience continues to feel vulnerable, helpless and oblivious to real interpersonal power. The patterns that lead to hysteria are also highlighted by Ortmeyer's (1979) observation that hysterics have mothers who do not allow autonomy. Hollender (1971) describes maternal deprivation with the substitution of the father for both parents, and Chapman and Chapman (1980) observe both indulgence and neglect.

Brisman (1992) applies interpersonal theory to the study of addiction, highlighting the paradoxical interpersonal impact of addiction or 'dependent avoidance'. Within the dependent avoidance framework the addict uses communication to deceive, control, or placate the other. Brisman also describes that the particular substance used by the addict to achieve the state of dependent avoidance is of less significance than the interpersonal structure it sets up. The addict typically sets up relationships that avoid the stress of intimacy while meeting the addict's dependency needs. Addiction is viewed as a defence against feelings of ineffectiveness. Such feelings originate in early family relationships that were precarious and unresponsive to the developing child's needs. As a result the child is overwhelmed by feelings of helplessness and ineffectiveness regarding the world. Temporary illusions of hope and control are then sought in adulthood in ritualized behaviour, such as gambling, which can provide the temporary illusion of hope and control. The focus in an interpersonal understanding of addiction is on when, how, and why the addict sets up interpersonal relationships characterized by both distance and dependency.

There is, however, controversy about the status of interpersonal approach within the psychoanalytical school. For example, Summers (1994 cited in Celani 1997) places it under the general title of object relations (a controversial matter in itself), while other theorists view it as outside the frame of reference of psychoanalysis. They point out the relative lack of consideration given by interpersonal theorists to core object relations concepts such as 'conflict' and 'the internal'.

Erik Erikson (1902–94)

Ego psychology introduced a significant departure from traditional psychoanalysis, since it represents a shift in focus from the id to the ego. One of its best-known proponents is Erikson. Whereas Freud outlined stages of psychosexual development, Erikson offers a psychosocial stage theory that emphasizes social tasks and associated conflicts throughout the lifespan (Erikson 1963). Each of Erikson's stages is dependent on the development of the preceding stage and the unfolding of each stage is based on two underlying basic assumptions. First, the steps are predetermined, so that the individual is ready to be motivated towards growth and development and prepared to interact with a widening social radius. Second, society tends to be constituted so as to encourage and safeguard the proper rate and sequence of the stages.

The eight stages range from the oral to late adulthood, with the issues in the eight ages being (in order) basic trust versus mistrust, autonomy versus shame and doubt, initiative versus guilt, industry versus inferiority, identity versus identity confusion, intimacy versus isolation, generativity versus stagnation and integrity versus despair. At each stage, there can be positive or negative outcomes. Erikson used the term 'identity crisis' to describe points in life where the person is between progression and regression. Successful resolution of the crisis promotes a particular virtue or strength at each stage. At the same time it can be seen how weakness in any of the virtues, or failure to negotiate the tasks of a particular age constitute risks in the 'structure' of the person, which under stress may lead to regression to that stage of development; or even to fixation at a particular stage, having not totally been able to leave it behind.

Erikson's model of ego psychology is different from Freud's psychoanalytical model in some significant respects. Whereas Freud emphasized the role of the id – instincts and conflicts are seen as central in shaping personality and psychopathology – ego psychology assumes that the ego functions not only as a defence against the workings of the id, but also that the ego strives for mastery of the environment and produces a separate and conflict free driving force towards adaptation to reality. The difference between the two approaches may be seen, for example, when considering Freud's latency period. Whereas Freud did not view this to be an important stage in personality development, Erikson stressed that this was the time where the individual strives to develop a sense of industry, the failure of which leads to a sense of inferiority. Failure and success at developing a sense of industry was largely determined by cultural forces because discrimination of race, gender and religion leads to some individuals growing up lacking a sense of industry (Erikson, 1963). In acknowledging the influence of socio-cultural factors on psychopathology, ego psychology perspectives show some similarity with the socio-cultural model and with some of the neo-Freudian approaches. Like neo-Freudian approaches Erikson emphasizes the importance of interpersonal factors in psychopathology.

Object relations theory

The psychoanalytical perspective becomes even more complex when we consider later developments that have increasingly diluted Freud's mechanistic emphasis. This is seen in object relations theory (Fairbairn 1941; Guntrip 1950; for an overview see Rayner 1993), which replaces the hydraulic model of the mind with one based on the mapping of internal and external relationships. The consequence of this shift has been profound. In the classical theory of Freud, neurotic behaviour was seen as a mechanical failure – the defence systems had broken down. In object relations theory the model has a different interpretive perspective, examining the real (or in Kleinian theory the phantasized) aspects of relationships in somewhat different ways (see also Laing 1960; Holland 1978). Different perspectives within the object relations model may be quite distinct from each other but there are some similarities. At the most general level the model refers to theories that view interpersonal relations as more central to human development than the influence of drives – although Klein's emphasis on aggression has all the hallmarks of a drive theory. Further, although again with some differences in Klein, object relations perspectives emphasize the view that early relationships are central to personality and the development of psychopathology (for example Fairbairn 1952; Kohut 1971; Kernberg 1976).

Summers (1994 cited in Celani 1997) outlines a broad category of theorists under the heading of object relations, which includes self psychology and interpersonal psychology. Significant contributors to the theories of the object relations include Fairbairn and Guntrip, Klein, Winnicott, Balint, Kernberg and Kohut, as well as the interpersonal school. He points to the conceptual similarity between the theoretical ideas of self psychology and those of many British object relations theorists. Although these traditions are distinct in many ways, nevertheless there are commonalities in their approaches, notably their rejection of classical drive theory.

However, Hirsch (1997 cited in Celani 1997) criticizes Summers' categorization, pointing out that interpersonal psychoanalysis differs along a number of dimensions from both self psychology and British object relations theory. He points out interpersonal theory and self psychology developed from entirely different traditions and totally independently. Hirsch prefers the term 'relational' to describe a broad category that subsumes the traditions of interpersonal psychoanalysis and self psychology.

Although Freud was mainly concerned with the id and control

over id processes as the core organizing principle for personality and psychopathology, later psychoanalytical theorists became more concerned with projective and introjective mechanisms. This is mostly associated with the work of Melanie Klein (1882–1960). In *The Psychoanalysis of Children* (1932), she outlines the developmental process through which children introject (incorporate) the values and images of important caregivers who are invested with strong emotional attachments. These object representations (introjected people) become incorporated within the child's ego leading the child as an adult to respond to the environment through the perspective of internalized figures from his or her past. Klein viewed infants as relating to others, first as part objects (e.g. the breast) and later as whole objects (e.g. the mother). Fantasies about these objects as well as actual experience influence personality development and psychopathology. Klein emphasizes the defence of splitting which occurs whatever the nature of the mother–infant relationship – this is more a nature approach. The defence of splitting is a protective mechanism in which part objects are viewed as either all good or all bad, because the infant is at first unable to incorporate the object representation fully. Psychopathology of the paranoid-schizoid type is therefore part of all human experience, not the result of environmental failure.

Klein's approach attracted many followers, especially in Britain although less so in the United States. Her work had a profound influence on other psychoanalysts, although Fairbairn developed his own version of object relations. In his paper *A Revised Psychopathology of the Psychoses and Psychoneuroses* (1941), he outlined his views that paranoid, compulsive, hysteric and phobic states are not the result of fixations at different levels of libido development, but different techniques which the ego uses for the solution of the same primitive conflict. The child's relationship towards objects, according to Fairbairn, follows a typical development from identification to object differentiation. Between the immature identification phase and the mature love phase there are transitional states characterized by ambivalence and splitting of objects into good and bad.

Fairbairn discusses the psychopathology of the transitional states as well as of the identification phase. The conflict between a tendency towards separation from the object and the longing to keep the inner object is the basis of the phobic attitude. The same conflict, perceived as a conflict between the tendencies towards expulsion and retention is said to be the basis of the compulsion neurosis. When it is perceived as a contrast between acceptance and refusal of an object, it is characteristic of hysteria. The paranoid state means 'repulsion of the external and acceptance of the internal objects'. All these states try to overcome the difficulties of the transitional period. However, in depression and schizophrenia there is a failure to break with the problems of infantile dependency. The danger remains that the needed objects may be destroyed or hurt, first by 'love', which means through the act of incorporation, and later by 'hatred', because the ambivalence towards the object also entails the subjective aim of destruction.

The object relations approach stresses the object-seeking core of human nature and views attachment as arising primarily from other motivations than the satisfaction of need. Repetition of troubled attachments is related to the human inclination to maintain even the worst self-object integrations rather than none at all. This is viewed as a better explanation for the tendency to repeat negative patterns than Freud's concept of the death instinct.

Perhaps one of the distinctive features of object relations theory is that it is not monolithic. Here we have only touched on some aspects of its contribution to psychopathology. We might also have explored Balint's (1968) concept of the 'basic fault', or Winnicott's distinction between privation (never having experienced anything good) and deprivation (having experienced it but having it taken away) and the influence of the latter on the anti-social tendency (1958: 306–15). Another rather different but influential development has been the work of John Bowlby (1969, 1973, 1980) which we describe in more detail in the next chapter.

Psychoanalysis and the wider dimension

Another theoretical and clinical paradigm emerged in the development of group therapy within a psychoanalytical framework, influenced by the social context of the time including the necessity during the Second World War of producing a cost-effective way of treating soldiers suffering from reactions to traumatic experiences. One of the first examples of this is seen in the work of Bion (1959) that led to new insights about group dynamics. In the development of group analysis the focus of enquiry centred on the group rather than the individual. The debate then began as to whether or not group therapy was indeed psychoanalysis; for example, Foulkes comments: 'Psychoanalysis is a biological theory which only very reluctantly has been pushed into being a social theory by the pressure of psychotherapy. Group therapy is not psychoanalysis' (1965: 25).

A wide and diverse range of social scientists have claimed a relation-ship to some versions of Freud's psychoanalytic approach or its derivatives. Clinical psychoanalysis is concerned with hermeneutics – insight and interpretation. Within sociology the functionalism of Talcott Parsons has links with psychoanalysis; but equally the neo-Marxian critical theorists (the 'Frankfurt School') applied the her-meneutic framework to social relationships. A bridge between clinical psychoanalysis and the latter can be found in a range of analysts who have applied psychoanalysis to societal understandings, for example, Fromm, Reich, Horney, Fenichel and Bion.

One of the most notable features of psychoanalysis in relation to the neo-Marxist critical theorists (the 'Frankfurt School') is its pure view of the alienated psyche, which exists as some sort of separate self-contained entity, uncontaminated by ideology. Their approach is based on two main aspects of Freudian psychoanalysis.

First, they view the idea of a conscious agent as some kind of bourgeois conceptualization. Second, they emphasize the psycho-analytical position based on the assumption that there is only one essential truth about the functioning of individuals, and that truth is centred on the sexual instincts and the constraints imposed on them by society, as outlined by Freud. Within this orthodox tradition, alternative versions of psychology, and even the cultural psychology strand within the psychoanalysis of Erikson, are rejected. While Freud is viewed as unswerving in his intellectual endeavour all later revi-sions or alternatives to psychoanalysis are rejected as wrong, or at best viewed as giving way to superficial concerns.

Freud clearly was not a revolutionary socialist. Although in *Civiliza-tion and its Discontents* (1930/64) he pointed to civilization in its generic sense as being responsible for psychopathology, he did not emphasize the specifically alienating character of a capitalist society. Nevertheless, some neo-Marxists in their idealization of classical psychoanalytical theory show an intolerance of other approaches to subjectivity. This may be seen for example in Kovel (1988) and in Jacoby's *Social Amnesia: A Critique of Contemporary Psychology from Adler to Laing* (1975). Jacoby rejects everybody both inside and outside the tradition of depth psychology not adhering unconditionally to Freud's views about biology and society and dismisses any alternative constructions of reality stating:

If the history of psychology is the history of forgetting, Adler was the first, but by no means the last to forget. His revision of psychoanalysis was a homemade remedy to assuage the pain of the unfamiliar: psychoanalysis. The notions that he, and the neo-Freudians, championed were borrowings from everyday prattle: the self, values, norms, insecurities and the like. They were offered as antidotes to Freud's illiberalism. Yet just this constituted Freud's strength: his refusal to bow to reigning wisdom. (Jacoby 1975: 44–5)

For other disciplines studying society, such as sociology and anthropology, psychoanalysis has provided a bridge between society and the inner lives of individuals. Within the field of sociology there are strong critics of the view that neurosis is caused by the constraining forces of civilization on the instinct (e.g. Wootton 1959), but equally strong supporters of psychoanalysis (e.g. Titmuss 1958). Additionally, there are some from within a depth psychology framework who have taken into account the reality of the political context of client and therapist. For example, the analytical psychologist Samuels in *The Political Psyche* (1995) examines the relationship between insights from psychodynamic traditions and knowledge about the social world that influences and constrains our experience. Similarly the clinical psychologist/sociologist Richards is concerned with the relationship between the inner world of individuals and the wider socio-political context within which therapeutic theory and practice are located (e.g. *Capitalism and Infancy* 1984; and *Disciplines of Delight* 1994). We explore aspects of this wider debate in Chapters 7 and 8.

Criticisms of psychoanalytic models

Freud's work took place at a particular contextual time and place – the sexually repressive context of nineteenth-century middle-class Vienna. His views were seen as radical at the time, as they challenged the prevailing assumptions about the nature of personality and psychological suffering. His ideas have become part of Western cultural heritage. However, Freud's theories have been criticized widely, the most frequent being that they are not scientific (Eysenck and Wilson 1973, Steele 1982 and Sutherland 1998).

Both the theories and therapies based on the psychodynamic model have been criticized for their lack of scientific rigour. For example, Steele states:

Unfortunately, Freud's belief that his work was science, and as such discovered the truth, and his stance that either someone was for or against him created a dogmatic system. He had not developed the critical consciousness necessary to see that psychoanalysis was a method which constructed a causal historical narrative, but that other methods . . . could formulate different and equally plausible scenarios. His insistence on orthodoxy kept his approach to enquiry from being either truly scientific or truly hermeneutic. (Steele 1982: 360)

Critics argue that Freud's theories are too vague to be put to the test of science (Fisher and Greenberg 1996; Sutherland 1998). The scientific process is based on the concept of falsification (Popper 1959). Thus scientific hypotheses should be formulated in a way that they are capable of refutation, that is, can be shown to be false. Although some psychoanalytical conjectures can be tested scientifically many of the concepts are complex and do not easily lend themselves to the process of falsification. However, just because an idea cannot be tested scientifically this does not mean that it is not true, only that it is not possible to provide evidence in support of it.

Evidence for the efficacy of therapeutic techniques developed out of psychodynamic approaches to psychopathology is equivocal. Some researchers point out that the scientific evidence is not convincing, and that findings are typically based on the study of a limited number of people (Eysenck and Wilson 1973). Even if there are other studies that appear to provide some evidence for the efficacy of brief psychodynamic therapies (Malan 1979; Crits-Christoph 1992; Anderson and Lambert 1995), these do not prove the validity of the psychopathological models that underpin them.

A second criticism of the psychoanalytical model is that it is mechanistic, individualistic and is tied to its medical roots. Admittedly the model takes an opposite stance to biological psychiatry, but whereas biological psychiatry tends to reduce psychological phenomena to biology, psychoanalysis tends to make everything a psychological matter – whether describing the biological or the social as well as the purely personal. For many people, there may well be Oedipal conflicts and their attendant neuroses underlying their distress but as the social cultural model of psychopathology highlights, the concerns of everyday life may have far more effect on people's mental health. The theory and practice of psychoanalysis ignores a consideration of social realities (see also Chapter 8).

A third criticism is that the psychoanalytical model does not address the effect of personal futures. This excludes a field of enquiry that may exert a profound influence on human conduct and distress experienced in the present. Much empirical research points out how our expectations and aspirations influence our present conduct.

The psychoanalytical model has been generally criticized for being reductionist as it reduces multiple realities experienced within complex social relationships, in the present and past, to one understood within a tightly limited version of hermeneutics. Although psychoanalysis has provided an illuminating and enriching variety of views and insights into the human condition within a hermeneutic framework, nevertheless the theory is always given precedence over the patient's own view about themselves and their experiences of their world. The patient's own constructions tend to be viewed as, for example, unanalysed conscious reflections and therefore, inadequate, incomplete or incorrect. Precedence is given to the analyst's viewpoint and interpretations. The analyst of whatever specific psychoanalytical school has a set of prepared theoretical constructs or hermeneutic formats that are imposed on clients. Psychopathology appears to dominate. This not only applies to Freud's classical psychoanalysis but also to later developments. Guntrip, for example, takes an essentially reductionist stance when he reduces homosexuality and prostitution to schizoid defences. The varied and interacting uncertainties of life tend to be reduced to single variable explanations. This criticism of reductionism can also be made of the behavioural model.

Some psychoanalysts have refuted this criticism. For example, Casement (1985) emphasizes the importance of resisting preconceptions, and cautions against the psychoanalyst imposing interpretations upon patients. He notes how Bion advised that each analytical session should be approached 'without desire, memory or understanding' (1985: 17).

The implicit superiority of the psychoanalyst is very different to the therapeutic position of person-centred therapy that involves being with, empathically and non-judgementally listening to and engaging with the unique experiences of patients. To allow each new patient to have a unique self-constructing story might lead to psychoanalysis turning into a form of phenomenology or existentialism, although some analysts have certainly taken this path, as seen for example in the work of R.D. Laing. Others, such as Lomas (1987), although retaining a broad allegiance to psychoanalysis, criticize its interpretive imperatives and emphasize direct knowledge of people through their unique narratives.

Conclusion

It is impossible to draw definitive conclusions about psychopathology from a psychoanalytic perspective. The legacy of Freud is that we have an understanding that unconscious motives and defence mechanisms influence human conduct, and that early childhood experiences influence later experiences and influence adult personality adjustment. Although to varying degrees, most would agree with this general view, the devil is in the detail. This chapter has inevitably had to compress extensive and complex discussions of the psychogenesis of different states of mind and presenting symptoms. The extensive body of psychoanalytical literature that addresses these issues suggests that, whatever the acknowledgement made to Freud in those enquiries, there are many ways of understanding human dilemmas and behaviours that go beyond his theories. Freud's ideas, and those of many who have take them forward have attracted many followers as well as critics.

Many in the scientific community argue that psychoanalysis is not amenable to hypotheses testing criteria such as refutation inherent in the paradigm of traditional empirical research. Others view the empirical paradigm as an inadequate scientific model not appropriate for the study of subjective human experience. Although evidence suggests that psychodynamic therapy can be helpful, it is open to debate whether this is because psychoanalytic therapists convey valuable insights to their patients about what their suffering means, or because psychoanalysis acts as a flashlight enabling each therapist and patient to find a particular road. Psychoanalytical theory has had an important influence in a wider range of disciplines concerned with psychopathology. It has inspired many developments in the study of psychopathology, one of which we examine in rather more detail in the next chapter.

CHAPTER 4

Attachment theory

One of the most influential developments based on the psycho-analytical model is attachment theory, based on the work of John Bowlby (1958, 1969/1982, 1973, 1980). Like psychoanalysts generally (Erikson 1963; Freud 1965; Winnicott 1965; Mahler, Pine and Bergman 1975), Bowlby emphasizes the importance of early relationships, in particular the way the child forms attachments. These early attachments shape experiences in later life, and can result in the development of different forms of psychopathology.

Central to Bowlby's theory is the significance of the mother (caretaker) child relationship and biological bases of attachment behaviour (1969). Most theories of child development, psycho-analytical, cognitive and behavioural-social learning approaches, emphasize the influence social relationships in childhood have on mental health and illness. However, it was not until Bowlby's work that the association between early child attachment relationships and the development of various forms of psychological disorders was highlighted.

He draws on a wide range of disciplines including evolutionary biology, ethnology, developmental psychology, cognitive science and control systems theory, formulating a theory that the mechanisms underlying the infant's tie to mother are based on evolutionary processes. This strong tie, evident especially when disrupted, results not from an associational learning process but rather from a biologically based desire for proximity that arises through the biological process of natural selection.

Both psychoanalytical and social learning models propose that the infant's relationship with the mother emerges as a result of associations with feeding (Freud 1910/1957; Sears, Maccoby and Levin 1957, 1959). However, Bowlby questioned the assumptions of the current secondary drive theories pointing to findings from animal studies such as Lorenz (1957), who noted that infant geese become attached to parents that did not feed them, and Harlow (1958) who observed that infant rhesus monkeys in times of stress, prefer contact comfort to food. Other evidence came from work such as Spitz who in the 1950s made a film entitled *Grief; a Peril in Infancy*, which graphically portrayed babies in a serious state of decline even though their physical needs were being met. Attachment theory highlights that we are social beings and that dependency during infancy is not just physical nor just caused by simple pleasurable associations. Systematic observations of human infants confirm that infants also become attached to people who do not feed them (Ainsworth 1967). Further, studies show that children become attached whether or not their parents are meeting their psychological or physical needs – for example they become attached to abusive mothers (Ainsworth 1967; Bowlby 1956; Harlow 1962). Bowlby commented on secondary drive theory: 'For example, were it true, an infant of a year of two should take readily to whomever feeds him, and this clearly is not the case' (1980: 650). Instead, he (1958, 1960) proposed an attachment theory model, outlining his ideas in a series of papers, later elaborated in the trilogy *Attachment and Loss* (1969/1982, 1973, 1980).

An underlying premise of Bowlby's approach is the evolutionary principle, evident in cross-species comparative studies in the fields of ethology and primate research, of the genetic transmission of species survival in infancy and childhood. He proposes that during the time when humans were evolving in 'the environment of evolutionary adaptedness', genetic selection favoured attachment behaviours because they increase the likelihood of child–mother proximity, which in turn increased the likelihood of protection and provided survival advantage: 'the ultimate outcome to be attained is always the survival of the genes an individual is carrying' (1969/1982: 56).

Attachment behaviours are organized into an 'attachment behavioural system'. Bowlby (1969/1982) again derived this concept from ethology to describe a species-specific system of behaviour that leads to certain predictable outcomes rather than viewing attachment as a by-product of any other process or drive. He outlines the connection of the attachment behavioural system with other behavioural systems such as the exploratory, fear, sociable and care-giving systems, arguing that if an infant is not attached to someone then this infant has fewer chances in developing skills for interacting with other people and also helping to prepare them physically, for example in developing mobility. Research has established a clear link between secure attachment and other developmental processes, in particular language development and exploratory behaviour (Stroufe 1988; Caruso 1989). Fraiberg provides a succinct summary: 'Attachment helps the child: attain full intellectual potential, become self-reliant, cope with stress and frustration; handle fear and worry; develop future relationships and reduce jealousy' (1980: 13).

The attachment system enables the infant to respond flexibly to internal and external cues when attempting to attain a goal. For example, the child considers any change in its mother's location and behaviour and other environmental changes when trying to maintain proximity to the mother and uses a flexible variety of attachment behaviours, depending on the circumstances. When a separation becomes too great in distance or time, the attachment system becomes activated and when the goal of optimum proximity is achieved it is terminated. Attachment is considered a normal and healthy characteristic throughout the lifespan, rather than a sign of immaturity to be outgrown. The experience of security is the goal of the attachment system, which is thus a regulator of emotional experience (Stroufe 1996). In this sense it lies at the heart of many forms of mental disorder.

The development of attachments

Bowlby suggests that as in other species there is a critical period for the development of attachments between the human infant and caregiver. Infants display an innate tendency to become attached to one particular individual, initially the mother or prime caregiver, later developing a hierarchy of attachments. He proposes (1969/1982) four stages of attachment during infancy.

His early work on attachment theory (1944) started with observations made when working in a home for maladjusted boys. He became convinced that major disruptions in the mother–child relationship are precursors of later psychopathology. He thought that if a child is deprived of the mother between 6 months and 5 years of age this would lead to emotional and relational difficulties in later life. If a child does not develop an attachment by the age of 2½years then s/he or she will be at risk of permanent emotional damage. He suggests that separation experiences in early childhood caused affectionless psychopathy, the inability to have deep feelings for others, and therefore the lack of meaningful personal relationships.

Early studies in attachment focused on the anxiety formed when a child is separated from the mother. Bowlby, along with his colleague James Robertson, observed that children experienced intense distress when separated from their mothers, even when fed and cared for by others. A predictable pattern emerged – one of angry protest followed by despair (Robertson and Bowlby 1952). During the 1940s and 1950s Bowlby and Robertson filmed children undergoing such separations to show the importance of the attachment relationship (Karen 1994). Children experienced the separations as a fundamental threat to their well-being. Their reactions included fear, anger and desperate efforts to find the missing parent, giving way to despair, sadness and withdrawal. The second phase 'despair' resulted from failure of protest to induce the return of the lost figure. The third phase 'detachment' occurred after a prolonged period of sadness, marked by subdued activity and a notable lack of joy or enthusiasm. The apparent 'detachment' is not a neutral wearing away of an attachment bond, but rather a defensive suppression of attachment responses that have failed for a long while to produce the lost figure.

Patterns of attachment in infancy

Bowlby was also influenced by cognitive theory, discussing the role within the attachment system of cognitive processes, such as object permanence, discrimination learning, selective attention and memory. Drawing on cognitive information theory, he proposed (1969/ 1982) that the organization of the attachment behavioural system involves cognitive components – specifically, mental representations of the attachment figure, the self and the environment, all of which are largely based on experience. His emphasis on real experiences differs from the views of Freud (and Klein) who emphasized the role of internal fantasies. According to Bowlby, these representations or 'internal working models' allow individuals to anticipate the future and make plans – the child then uses these models, for example, when deciding which specific attachment behaviour to use in a specific situation. Conscious processing is needed in checking and revising the models. Extensive work has been carried out on these models (see reviews in Bretherton 1990 and Baldwin 1992).

These early experiences of attachment form the basis for infants' mental model of how relationships operate and act as a template or internal working model for relationships later on in life (Bowlby 1969/ 1982). When experiences lead to a 'confident expectation' (Winnicott 1971) that caregivers will be lovingly responsive, infants develop a model of the self as loved and valued, and a reciprocal model of the other. This confidence allows infants to develop secure strategies for seeking out their caregivers when distressed or in need, with the expectation that needs will be met. When infants instead have experiences that lead them to expect caregivers to be rejecting or undependable, they develop a model of the self as unloved or rejected, and a model of the other as unloving or rejecting. They do not expect that caregivers will be available when needed and they develop alternative, insecure strategies for coping with their distress. Insecure strategies vary primarily along the dimension of attempts to minimize or maximize the expression of attachment needs. Both of these strategies leave children at greater risk for psychopathology.

Bowlby also drew attention to individual and cultural differences in attachment behaviour.

Individual differences

Mary Ainsworth (1969, 1975, 1985) conducted studies exploring infants actively searching for contact with their mother. She developed a procedure for observing the infant's internal working model in action called the 'Strange Situation' technique in which the interaction between mothers and infants was observed prior to, during and after a brief separation. She demonstrated how infants, briefly separated from their caregiver in an unfamiliar situation, can be categorized as being secure or insecure, and show one of three basic patterns of attachment.

1. *Secure attachment style*   Secure infants cry relatively little unless the mother is absent and respond positively to being picked up. They are attached to mothers who are responsive and sensitive. They become distressed, protesting at the caregiver's brief absence, seek her out and greet her with delight when she returns. They are more active and curious, and interact well with strangers.

Insecurely attached infants show two different styles of behaviour:

2. *Anxious-ambivalent style*   These infants are highly distressed by the separation with the mother and more angry with her on her return.

They have great difficulty in settling when reunited with their mother and attempts at comforting fail to reassure.

3. *Avoidant style* These infants show relative indifference to the mother. They rarely cry when left and show little positive response on her return. They interact more coolly with their mother.

Longitudinal research demonstrates that children with a history of secure attachment are independently rated as more resilient, self-reliant, socially oriented (Stroufe 1983), empathic to distress (Kestenbaum et al. 1989), and make deeper relationships (Stroufe et al. 1990). A secure parent–child relationship encourages an autonomous sense of self (Emde and Buchsbaum 1990; Lieberman and Pawl 1990; Fonagy et al. 1995), and an empathic understanding of others (Stroufe 1990; Fonagy et al. 1995). Numerous empirical findings indicate that the development of a secure attachment with caregivers in the first two years of life is related to higher sociability with other adults and children, higher compliance with parents, and more effective emotional regulation (Ainsworth et al. 1978; Bretherton 1985; Richters and Waters 1991). Negative emotions feel less threatening, and can be experienced as meaningful and communicative (Stroufe 1979; Grossman et al. 1986; Stroufe 1996).

Disruptions in attachment relationships

Insecure attachment before 2 years of age has been related to lower sociability, poorer peer relations, symptoms of anger and poorer behavioural self-control from pre-school onwards (Carlson and Stroufe 1995). Bowlby (1973, 1980) suggests that when children develop negative representations of self or others, or when they adopt strategies for processing attachment-related thoughts and feelings that compromise realistic appraisals, they become more vulnerable to psychopathology.

Crittenden (1988) further developed attachment patterns identifying a fourth category: avoidant/ambivalent. Children in this group become compulsively compliant, and inhibit signals of displeasure even in situations that warrant protest. Further, she links attachment patterns to style of mothering:

- securely attached children tend to have sensitive mothers;
- anxious/ambivalent children tend to have unresponsive mothers;
- anxious/avoidant children tend to have unresponsive and controlling mothers;

• avoidant/ambivalent children tend to have highly controlling mothers.

Studies have elaborated Ainsworth's original categories to include more severe forms of reaction such as disorganization and disorientation. Infants in this group react to separation with, for example, freezing, or head banging (see Main and Solomon 1990). Not surprisingly, a history of severe neglect or physical or sexual abuse is often associated with this pattern (Cicchetti 1983; Main and Hesse 1990). Main and Solomon (1986) explored disorganized attachment in infancy and adulthood. They discovered that although some infants who have been unpredictably frightened by their attachment figures may display the typical secure and insecure attachment strategies many show temporary lapses in their strategies, marked by fear, freezing and disorientation. They proposed a new classification of 'disorganized-disoriented', for infants showing these behaviours.

The stability of attachment is demonstrated by longitudinal studies of infants followed up in adolescence and adulthood. Studies (Hamilton 1994; Waters et al. 1995; George et al. 1996; Main 1997) have shown a 68–75 per cent correspondence between attachment classifications in infancy and classifications in adulthood. For example, George et al. (1996) used a measure classifying individuals as Secure/Autonomous, Insecure/Dismissing, Insecure/Preoccupied or Unresolved with respect to loss or trauma. Autonomous individuals value attachment relationships, coherently integrate memories into a meaningful narrative and regard these as formative. Insecure individuals are poor at integrating memories of experience with the meaning of that experience. Those dismissive of attachment show avoidance by denying memories and idealizing and/or devaluing early relationships. Preoccupied individuals tend to be confused, angry or passive in relation to attachment figures, often still complaining of childhood slights, echoing the protests of the resistant infant. Unresolved individuals give indications of significant disorganization in their attachment relationship representation in semantic or syntactic confusions in their narratives concerning childhood trauma or a recent loss.

Research (Fraiberg 1980; Main 1996) also suggests that attachment patterns can be transmitted across generations, playing a key role in the transgenerational transmission of deprivation. Secure adults are three or four times more likely to have children who are securely attached to them (van Ijzendoorn 1995). It is assumed that securely attached adults are more sensitive to their children's needs and respond appropriately (Belsky et al. 1995; De Wolff & van Ijzendoorn 1997).

Over the last decade or so much follow-up data has been accumulated on attachment theory showing a connection between secure attachment and later development. Bretherton and Waters's (1985) study of 6-year-olds indicated that securely attached children were more able to cope with parental absence and related to unfamiliar adults more readily. Insecurely attached children were anxious, tongue-tied and rejecting of their parents. Others have identified a link between insecure attachments and conduct problems and long-term consequences of avoidance (Belsky and Nezworski 1988). Studies have explored the relationship between attachment-relevant events in childhood (for example trauma and separation from parents) and later psychopathology, and the relationship between concurrently assessed 'attachment styles' (the individual's self-reported style of forming adolescent and adult attachments) and psychopathology (Hazan and Shaver 1987, 1994). There is also much research evidence linking attachment behavioural strategies in infancy with adult psychopathology. More recent theoretical contributions and empirical research have expanded on Bowlby's original conceptualizations and established the current interest in attachment as a core construct in child development and psychopathology. Fonagy (1999) outlines how the child's experience and representation of secure attachment is internalized by the child to form part of the self. Lieberman and Zeanah (1995) illustrate how atypical attachment patterns in the first years of life may themselves be considered early disorders.

The role of attachment in the development of psychopathology

Bowlby formulated a model of development with clearly articulated implications for psychopathology. In his 1973 volume, he highlights how threats to the availability of attachment figures, together with defensive processes and distorted communication within the parent–child relationship, can result in symptomatic expressions of fear, anger and sadness. From infancy specific emotions accompany an individual's appraisal of the availability of an attachment figure. These emotions normally serve important motivational, self-monitoring and communication functions for the individual (Bowlby 1969/1982). He also illustrates (1973) how attachment processes contribute to childhood anxiety disorders and phobias. Anxiety can be considered the fundamental condition underlying insecure attachment. He distinguishes between 'true phobias' (in which a child is afraid of something in the environment, such as spiders or snakes) and 'pseudo-phobias' (such as school refusal or agoraphobia). Bowlby suggests, that unlike true phobias, these may be better understood as resulting from the absence or feared loss of an attachment figure. Thus fear and worry about the availability of the attachment figure may result in a child's staying home to monitor the parent closely. He nevertheless leaves open the possibility that phobias may develop through conditioning and avoidance learning.

Bowlby (1973) proposes that when children experience separations from parents, and when parents threaten abandonment, they feel intense anger. Ordinary but stressful separations are often met with anger, which is functional in communicating to the parents the children's feelings about the separation. He reports several studies indicating increased anger and hostility following a prolonged separation. However, when prolonged separations are combined with frightening threats, or when caregivers misread the anger and respond with more anger or with disengagement, then children often feel intense hate. Bowlby suggests that this might become destructive and dysfunctional for the child. Initially the anger may be directed toward the parents. However, because that may prove dangerous in maintaining the relationship with the parent, the child's anger is often repressed and directed toward other targets (Stott 1950; Bowlby 1973), such as peers (George and Main 1979).

Fear and anger are evident when the child protests to the threat of availability of the attachment figure, whereas sadness tends to appear as the child begins to accept the loss. Withdrawal is the behaviour that normally accompanies sadness and this disengagement provides time to adapt to unwelcome changes and revise working models. Detached response to separation represents an attempt to downplay attachment feelings. Bowlby views this as a defensive effort to deactivate the attachment system and thus gain control over the painful emotions. Although this gives children a way of coping with anxious and angry feelings, it leads to difficulties when reunited with parents. Detached children show cool neutrality towards parents and an apparent apathy. Attachment-related feelings of sadness and despair may become more pervasive depressive symptoms; attachment-related fears may be expressed as anxiety disorders or dissociative symptoms; and attachment-related anger might appear in aggressive and antisocial behaviours. Emotions no longer serve as signals that facilitate understanding and communication, and instead become symptoms that appear puzzling and problematic (Kobak et al. 1994).

Bowlby (1980) suggests three major types of circumstances that are most likely to be associated with later development of depression. First, when a child's parent dies, and the child experiences little control over ensuing circumstances, s/he is likely to develop a sense of hopelessness and despair in reaction to traumatic events. Second, when a child is unable, despite many attempts to form stable and secure relationships with caregivers, s/he develops a model of the self as a failure. Any subsequent loss or disappointment is then likely to be perceived as reflecting that the child is a failure. Third, when a parent conveys to the child that s/he is incompetent or unlovable, the child develops complementary models of the self as unlovable and of the other as unloving (Bretherton 1985). Thus the child and later the adult will expect hostility and rejection from others when in need.

Attachment-related circumstances such as separation and loss can lead to different current and later manifestations of distress. Loss predicts multiple disorders, including depression, anxiety and anti-social personality disorder. To some degree, the type of loss experienced appears to affect the development of psychopathology differentially. Depression is associated generally with the early loss of the mother. Brown and Harris's (1978) work on depression (see Chapter 7 of this book), suggests that major depression is related to permanent loss of a caregiver, whereas depression characterized by anger and other externalizing symptoms is related to separation. Anxiety appears to be associated more closely with threats of loss and instability than with permanent loss (Monroe and Simons 1991) and divorce (McCord 1979). In his first empirical study, Bowlby (1946) argued that the loss of a primary attachment figure was a predisposing factor in juvenile delinquency. Anti-social personality disorder is associated with loss through desertion or separation. Although Bowlby's ideas about loss changed and developed over the course of his career, he continued to view the loss of an attachment figure as a major factor in personality development, and unresolved and suppressed grief as an important pathogenic force.

Secure attachment provides an element of protection during periods of high stress. Recent studies illustrate how the management of anxiety, anger and sadness through the healthy use of secure-base figures and mature defences is likely to be an important protective factor against various forms of psychopathology across the lifespan (Carlson and Stroufe 1995; Fonagy et al. 1995; Main 1996; Dozier et al. 1999; Kobak 1999).

Bowlby (1973) uses the metaphor of 'branching railway lines' to describe the development of psychopathology and psychological health. Infants with emotionally available caregivers take a different developmental path from those with emotionally unavailable caregivers. Future experiences with caregivers, and experiences of loss and abuse have differential effects on these children because they are on different branching pathways (Stroufe 1997). Certain pathways become more or less likely because there evolves within a child an organized system for coping with his or her experiences (Stroufe 1996). Patterns of anxious attachment represent initiation of pathways that if pursued increase the likelihood of a psychological condition. Thus although anxious attachment is considered a risk factor, not all anxiously attached infants develop a psychopathology. Psychopathology, according to this model is determined developmentally, involving a myriad of influences interacting over time (Stroufe 1997). Similarly secure attachment is no guarantee of mental health, but is a protective factor. Children with secure histories are more resistant to stress (Pianta et al. 1990) and more likely to rebound toward adequate functioning following a period of troubled behaviour (Stroufe et al. 1990).

The core emotional reactions that accompany threats to the availability of an attachment figure remain similar across the lifespan, and maintaining access to an attachment figure continues to be the goal of the attachment system from infancy to adulthood. As the individual matures, access turns on the individual's cognitive appraisals of the availability of the attachment figure (Bowlby 1973; Ainsworth 1990).

Three points may be made when considering the implications of the process of attachment to adult psychopathology. First, disruptions in attachment relationships that threaten availability result in anxious feelings, and if confidence is not restored, in anxious/insecure attachments. Research suggests that attachment security from childhood to adulthood remains a central relationship construct (Stroufe and Fleeson 1986). Second, although internal working models are resistant to change and are carried forward into new relationships, these working models bias but do not determine appraisals of an attachment figure's availability. This suggests that a person may experience variability in the security of a relationship, depending on the behaviour of a current attachment partner. Third, working models must be updated and revised to accommodate to new relationships (Bowlby 1980). Thus, attachment security results from a dynamic transaction between internal working models and the quality of current attachment relationships.

The evidence specifically linking infant attachment behavioural strategies to psychopathology in adulthood is illustrated by longitudinal studies (Lyons-Ruth 1996; Warren et al. 1997; Carlson 1998). Evidence that the emotions of fear, anger and sadness persist as responses to disruptions in adult attachment relationships comes from Weiss's 1975 study of individuals who were dissolving their marriages. There is also strong evidence for problematic family conditions in the development of borderline personality disorders, with very high rates of prolonged separations from caregivers during childhood (Ammaniti et al. 1998), especially from mothers (Soloff and Millward 1983). They also report emotional neglect when their caregivers were physically present (Patrick et al. 1994). People with borderline personality disorders are characterized by a very unstable sense of self and unstable, undeveloped representations of others who may be alternatively valued and devalued (American Psychiatric Association 1994).

Similarly many studies point to the relationship between childhood attachment related experiences and later anti-social personality disorder. For example, McCord (1979) and Robins (1966) found that parental desertion, divorce or separation was associated with later anti-social personality disorder. Zanarini et al. (1989) found that 89 per cent of persons with anti-social personality disorder had experienced prolonged childhood separations from caregivers.

Although Bowlby was primarily concerned with understanding infant-caregiver attachment, he conceptualized adult pair–bond relationships within the same theoretical framework (Bowlby 1969/1982; Parkes and Weiss 1983). One of his most important contributions is to understanding bereavement, the function and course of mourning and patterns of 'disordered' mourning, found in Bowlby's volume *Loss* (1980). He outlines four phases of mourning in adults – numbing; yearning and anger; disorganization and despair; reorganization. He describes how seemingly irrational or immature reactions to loss, such as disbelief, anger, searching and sensing the continued presence of the lost attachment figure are understandable when viewed from an attachment theory perspective. The absence of an attachment figure activates an innate motivational system that compels the individual to search for the lost person and do everything possible to regain that person's proximity and care. When these efforts fail, the bereaved person experiences profound sorrow and despair. Eventually the bereaved individual reorganizes his or her representations of the world in a way that allows him to return to normal activities and seek out or renew social relationships. Bowlby also proposes a framework for conceptualizing atypical mourning lying along a single conceptual dimension running from 'chronic mourning' to 'prolonged absence of conscious grieving' (1980: 138). There is considerable empirical support for his idea that chronic mourning stems from an anxious-ambivalent attachment organization. As a result, when irretrievable losses occur, anxious-ambivalent or preoccupied individuals have difficulty resolving these losses because their attachment systems are primed to continue yearning and searching for the missing attachment figures (see also Parkes and Weiss 1983; Main and Hesse 1990).

In contrast, absence of grief is characterized by a conspicuous lack of conscious sorrow, anger or distress. An individual may express relatively little distress following the loss, continue in their job and other activities without any noticeable disruption, and seek little support or solace from friends or family. 'Compulsive self-reliance' stems from early attachment experiences where the expression of emotion was discouraged.

As this section has illustrated, Bowlby's attachment theory and later developments from it have clear implications for the development of psychopathology. Attachment as a lifespan phenomenon is seen in his earliest writings (1956); and while his main focus was the early mother–child relationship, and most of the early research focused on infant development in normal settings (Main 1996), researchers have now applied attachment theory to understand and treat manifestations of distress, in which relationship factors are a cause (Ciccetti et al. 1995). Bowlby's own background in psychoanalysis is reflected in his emphasis on the significance of childhood in understanding later psychopathology. However, his work draws upon other disciplines marking his work out as distinct from that of his psychoanalytical colleagues many of whom were suspicious of the behavioural aspects of his theory. While Bowlby did not set out to bridge the divide between the psychoanalytic and the behavioural models, his work draws upon both, making the place of this chapter an appropriate one, separating two traditionally opposing models.

Behavioural, cognitive and cognitive-behavioural models

Behavioural psychology is nearly as contemporaneous as psycho-analysis as a psychological discipline although it developed later as a form of therapy. Behaviourism, like all models developed within a wider social and academic context. Both the psychoanalytical and behavioural models have in different ways been influenced in their formation and development by their relationship with the medical model. Regarding their considerations of psychopathology, the psychoanalytical and behavioural model are similar in that both con-sider concepts of normality as well as abnormality and share many diagnostic terms, although using different causal frameworks.

The dominant models of psychopathology until the First World War were based on the predominant philosophical considerations of the time which were those of evolutionary biology. The primary model of mental health was the biological model of bio-determinism which viewed mental disorder as well as any other form of deviance as resulting from some inherited weakness, or because of bad genes rather than because of any environmental or experiential influence. Mental disorder was conceptualized as a biological fault and those defined as mad were segregated into asylums and treated by medical doctors.

This bio-determinist tradition provided the context within which the later development of psychology as an academic discipline took place. This is seen, for example in the work of Sir Francis Galton (1857–1911), whose theories were influential in the development of British psychology.

The ascendancy of the Galtonian tradition with its emphasis on hereditary rather than environmental factors influencing human behaviour fitted well into the social context of the time with its emphasis on regulating and classifying certain sections of the population. Psychologists developed a psychometric testing role in personality and intelligence testing. A major influence was the development by Galton (1869) and Karl Pearson (1857–1936) of statistical and psychometric methodology and terminology that gave credibility to the new profession claiming status as a positivist science concerned with facts. The other main contextual factor which influenced future views of mental health was the effect of the two world wars. During this period psychological models gained acceptance as it became clear that bio-determinist theories were inadequate for explaining problems of low morale and fear. A vacuum was left in which other models, including psychotherapies based on Freud's work, developed which were not just concerned with the control of mental disorder but with the alleviation of emotional distress. This period facilitated new psychological models of psychopathology based on methodological behaviourism. Behaviour therapy, with its emphasis on a scientific approach, was also ideally suited to be the vehicle whereby clinical psychology changed its focus from psychometrics in the 1950s to the practice of therapy in the scientist-practitioner model as advocated by Eysenck (1958). For example, Shapiro (1963) emphasized the application of experimental psychology to clinical case studies. The model of the scientist diagnostician also fitted well into the existing psychiatric model, providing a shared scientific language in which to conduct research.

The birth of academic psychology was thus influenced by the academic traditions of the time, an empirical positivist legacy, emphasizing objective science with detached scientists applying the laws of behaviour to human subjects. Theories and models that did not fit into this rigid scientific view of the world, such as psychoanalysis and most verbal therapies, were rejected as being woolly and unscientific.

Scientifically respectable psychology became conceived as the science of behaviour, which was understood to include only the observable activities of an organism. As a school of thought it was inaugurated by the American psychologist J.B. Watson during the First World War and developed further after the Second World War, especially by B.F. Skinner. In the behaviourist model, observable behaviour is studied but ideas, feelings, thoughts, and so on are deemed insignificant in the attempt to eliminate all reference to subjective experience. Data are accordingly restricted to the observable reactions produced by observable stimuli. The behaviourist aims to understand the laws relating a stimulus to a response, how responses are built up into complex behaviours and how conditioning affects behaviour. The approach has been successful in describing how animals learn tasks in the laboratory, but cannot fully account for such complex processes as emotion, language and interpersonal relationships. Watson (1913) viewed human development as a mechanical process. He conceptualized the complete personality, as meaning the whole system of overt behaviours, built up out of the conditioning process. Although contemporary learning theorists, as we shall see later in this chapter, have developed and elaborated on the original model of the processes of behaviour acquisition and behaviour change, this simple model remains one of the cornerstones of behaviourism and continues to exert a powerful influence. As Watson wrote:

> Give me a dozen healthy infants, well-formed, and my own specified world to bring them up in and I'll guarantee to take any one at random and train him to become any type of specialist I might select – doctor, lawyer, artist, merchant-chief, and yes, even beggar-man and thief, regardless of his talents, penchants, tendencies, abilities, vocations, and race of his ancestors. (1925: 82)

Skinner developed the model in his concept of Radical Behaviourism. Behaviour was expanded to 'private events' like thinking, and feeling, which even though not observable were taken to be kinds of behaviour, subject to the same laws as more conspicuous behaviour. Skinner pointed out that despite the fact that there are private psychological events, psychology can avoid talking about them and thus retain its scientific credential. Assuming that unobservable private events operate according to similar laws, we can for purposes of psychology treat the mind like a black box, observing the effect of the environment on behaviour, and so predict and explain behaviour on that basis.

In *Behaviourism at 50* Skinner writes: 'It is especially important that a science of behaviour face the problem of privacy. It may do so without abandoning the basic position of behaviourism. Science often talks about things we can not see or measure. The skin is not that important a boundary.' In his radical behaviourism, Skinner argued that behaviour, public or private, is governed by the laws of classical conditioning (defined by Pavlov and Watson) or operant conditioning (as defined by Thorndike and himself). Skinner viewed that thinking, choosing, and deciding – things about which the stricter forms of behaviourism had vowed silence – could be analysed as private behaviours with characteristic causal relations to overt behaviour and as subject to the basic principles of operant conditioning. Despite this expanded view, Skinner remained unimpressed with the rising tide of cognitive psychology. Behaviourism, the theory that tried to limit the view of psychology to behaviour and eliminate subjective experience as data, is still prevalent in psychology although it is no longer the central or only model. However, behaviour therapy and its modified versions are still common practices. Consequently, many psychologists are concerned to operationalize in behavioural terms what they mean by psychopathology or abnormality. Terms such as 'maladaptive behaviour' 'unwanted' or 'unacceptable behaviour' are still part of this vocabulary. The strength of this position is that it makes explicit its criteria for what constitutes abnormality.

Learning and conditioning

Just as the psychoanalytic perspective developed partly through dissatisfaction with the narrowness of a biological model of psychopathology, the behavioural model developed partly because psychologists found the psychoanalytic model unscientific and ineffective. The behaviour model is constructed on the work of learning theorists. Behaviourists thought that the same behaviours that Freud studied could be explainable in a simpler fashion, in ways that would make them experimentally testable within a scientific framework.

Although both the psychoanalytical and the behavioural models are deterministic they locate the source of determinism in a different place. Whereas Freud located the source of human conduct in intrapsychic events, learning theorists view behaviour as a product of stimulus-response (S-R) relationships. Hence, in this model there is no need to explore the past or to understand the reasons for present behaviour in order to bring about change.

In learning theory, a change in behaviour is brought about by changing the relevant aspects of the environment, in particular by changing the different sources of reinforcement. A reinforcer is an event the occurrence of which will increase the probability that a particular stimulus will evoke a particular response. Reinforcers reward the individual for doing the right thing or for not doing the wrong thing. As long as the reward is desirable enough, the person will keep on behaving that way as long as the response continues to be reinforced. The response can either be an approach response (for example asking for more food) or an escape response (for example running away from a loud noise, or refusing to go out at night). Positive reinforcement is used to establish a specific behaviour or behaviours and increases the likelihood that the desired response will be made by giving the individual a reward or reinforcer that is desired. One example of this is giving a child sweets when he or she finishes a homework project; or saying 'well done' when a child finishes a task. The basic paradigm here is: Response – Reinforcement – Increased probability that the response will be repeated. In a similar way, when parents are teaching a child to speak, parents reward the child with smiles and hugs whenever it says a desired word like 'mummy'. These parental behaviours are positive reinforcements; they increase the probability that the child will speak that word again.

Negative reinforcement is used to establish any behaviour by removing an aversive stimulus when the behaviour occurs. A negative reinforcer thus increases the likelihood that the desired response will be made, but this time by taking away something that has been experienced as unpleasant when the behaviour previously occurred. An example of this is ceasing to tell off a child when he or she picks up a toy that they have thrown across the room. Another way of changing behaviour is through punishment. Punishment is an aversive stimulus that is given as a result of an unwanted behaviour to try and stop that behaviour occurring in the future. This essentially entails giving an unpleasant consequence to an individual for making the wrong response, for example, sending a child to her room for hitting her brother. Extinction entails suppressing behaviour by removing the reinforcers that are maintaining it, for example, by ignoring a child who is having a temper tantrum.

Although what we have described overlaps with the therapeutic methods of behaviourism it highlights an important factor pertinent to the aetiology of psychopathology, that through reinforcers of one sort or another – perhaps reinforcers that have had a negative effect – the child or adult has learned certain behaviours. Learning theorists view human behaviour as complex only in so far that even the simplest act can be considered as a chain of responses, each of which needs to be learned. In terms of human development, learning theorists point out that children usually need more than one trial at a particular task before learning takes place. Thus, learning theorists emphasize the process of 'shaping' as one of the basic processes in child development. This means reinforcing a successively better approximation of a desired behaviour in order to achieve the goal of establishing the desired response.

Classical and operant conditioning

The use of the basic learning theory of reinforcement on research on maladaptive behaviour has followed two general paradigms – that of classical conditioning and that of operant conditioning. Classical conditioning is essentially a process of learning by temporal association. The response that an organism automatically makes to a certain stimulus is transferred to a new stimulus through an association made between the two stimuli. We then come to respond to one as we do to the other. In a study that Pavlov (1928) was carrying out on the digestive system of dogs, he noticed that after a while the dogs began to salivate when the researchers were about to feed the dogs. Later it was noticed that the dogs began to salivate when they heard the footsteps of the researchers coming to feed them. Pavlov went on to test this observation by ringing a bell before the food was brought, finding that the dogs came to associate the sound of the bell with the food and would begin to salivate. In another experiment, Pavlov placed a hungry dog in a harness and turned a light on at certain intervals. At this point the dog did not salivate in response to the light, which was the conditioned stimulus (CS). However, after a few trials, meat powder was given to the dog directly after the light was switched on. As the dog was hungry it salivated – an unconditioned response (UR) – on presentation of the unconditioned stimulus (US), the meat powder. After several trials when meat powder was given to the dog after the light was turned on, Pavlov observed that the dog salivated when the light was turned on even if the meat powder was not given to the dog. Thus, a conditioned response (CR) to the light had been established.

Although seemingly a simple process, classical conditioning has far-reaching implications for understanding some forms of psychopathology, leading in turn to the development of therapeutic interventions within this framework. The behavioural model suggests that maladaptive behaviour or psychopathology can develop as a result of classical conditioning and that through modifying environmental stimuli, psychopathology can be extinguished. The basic paradigm of classical conditioning has been put forward as a framework for explaining a number of psychological problems such as fears, anxieties and other types of emotional reactions. In particular, classical conditioning is now generally accepted as an explanation as to why some people develop phobias. Many of these psychological reactions can develop because of accidental classical conditioning. For example, a child who has been bitten by a dog may come to fear all dogs and through generalization, other types of animals. The earliest study to show this was carried out by J.B. Watson (1878–1958) who is credited with recognizing the importance of classical conditioning as an explanation for psychological problems. Watson and Rayner (1920) first introduced an 11-month-old boy called Little Albert to a tame rat. At first, Albert was not fearful of the rat and would reach out and touch it. However, the researchers then startled Albert by striking a hammer on steel, which made a loud noise whenever he reached out to touch the rat. Over a period of several days this process was repeated with Watson and Rayner observing the boy's reaction. After a while Albert showed fear of the rat and would no longer reach out to touch it. Further, his fear spread to include other objects similar to the white rat such as a white rabbit and cotton wool. Watson showed that fears can be conditioned, thereby laying the foundations for behaviour therapy for phobias.

Wolpe and Rachman (1960) point out that classical conditioning can explain all our fears, because any neutral stimulus, whether simple or complex, that makes an impact on a person at about the same time as the fear reaction is evoked, is later able to produce a fear response. However, it should be pointed out that not only is the Little Albert study ethically questionable but also later work has not always been able to replicate the Little Albert study and it has been suggested that early writers on conditioning tended to ignore negative research findings in their eagerness to replace psychoanalysis with a science of behaviour (Samelson 1980).

Operant conditioning follows the American psychologist Edward Thorndike's (1874–1949) 'law of effect' (1898). In this paradigm, responses become more frequent if followed by satisfying consequences, but less frequent if followed by aversive consequences.

Whereas classical conditioning is concerned with the pairings of an unconditional stimulus with a conditional stimulus to produce behaviour, operant conditioning or instrumental conditioning is a process that is concerned with how that behaviour is maintained. Thorndike noted that when something positive happens we tend to repeat what we were doing, and when something negative happens we tend not to repeat it. Thorndike demonstrated this process by placing a cat in a box that was designed so that the cat had to press a lever to escape from the box. The cat was then deprived of food and a piece of fish was placed just outside the box where the cat could see it. Thorndike observed how, although at first the cat's behaviour was erratic as it tried to find a way out of the box, the cat would eventually press the lever, escape and get the fish. The next time the cat was put in the box, the time it took to press the lever was shorter, and the next time shorter still. Eventually, the cat on entering the box would very quickly press the lever and escape. Thorndike reasoned that when responses lead to positive consequences, in this case getting the fish, those responses are strengthened and the more likely to occur in the future. However, when responses lead to negative consequences the responses are not strengthened and are less likely to occur in the future. This is termed the law of effect, and became a theoretical cornerstone of behavioural psychology. B.F. Skinner (1904–90) coined the term operant conditioning to describe the process outlined by Thorndike. He elaborated on the relationship between instrumental behaviour and its consequences, for example, showing that when a rat is rewarded for acting on its environment, it will increase those actions, that is, it has associated the stimulus (reinforcement) with its own behaviour (response). This is known as S-R conditioning.

Operant behaviour is controllable and voluntary and can be conditioned by positive reinforcement and negative reinforcement. Various psychological problems have been approached from the behavioural perspective. Classical conditioning helps explain the formation of maladaptive behaviour and operant conditioning its persistence.

Mowrer (1947) proposed the two-factor model of fear and avoidance, in which fear was acquired through classical conditioning (first factor) and maintained through operant conditioning via negative reinforcement (second factor) as the person avoids their fear. Behaviourists point out that as learning contingencies operate over time, complex behaviour patterns are slowly shaped from childhood onwards (Gewirtz and Pelaez-Nogueras 1992). These processes can clearly be applied to understanding the psychopathology of certain behaviours.

Social learning theory

Social learning theorists point out that although the environment influences our behaviour, through our behaviour we can also influence the environment, and argue that although environmentalism may explain the behaviour of pigeons and laboratory rats, it cannot adequately explain the complexity of human behaviour and the factors that differentiate the human species from other less complex species. They emphasize that a number of factors combine in shaping the social behaviour and the mental state of the individual, and that such factors mediate the influence of learning experiences. One of the most influential social learning theorists was Albert Bandura, who carried out work on modelling in the learning process. This involves learning behaviour through watching others, that is, learning by imitation (Bandura and Walters 1963; Bandura 1969).

Freud (1940/1969) also discusses the process of learning through identification and how children usually come to identify with the same sex parent. In a series of studies conducted by Bandura, children watched adults behaving in either an aggressive or non-aggressive way. Then the children were allowed to play and it was found that those children who had watched the aggressive adults were more likely to play in an aggressive way than those children who had watched the adults behaving non-aggressively. The observed behaviour may be stored and used at a later date when a similar situation to the one in which the original modelling took place occurs. The therapeutic method that arises from this view is that of modelling – a process by which behaviour is changed because we are able to learn by observing how others do things.

Learning theorists point out that exposure to role models whose behaviour and skills we admire plays a crucial part in personal development. From the viewpoint of society, models may have a positive effect or a negative effect; for example, clinical studies point out that observational learning plays a part in the acquisition of maladaptive behaviour (Sarason and Sarason 1984). Anxiety in patients may be traced back to modelling experiences. A phobia may represent an exaggeration of a major or minor fear that a developing child has observed in a parent. Likewise a child may learn that aggression is the best way to deal with a dispute if one of the parents copes with frustration with violence. Learning theorists take the view that watching television or a video is basically a symbolic modelling experience, especially for children. They conclude that there is a link between aggression displayed on television and aggressive behaviour in viewers. However, some studies point out that this is not a simple direct causal relationship, since there is more likely to be a link if the viewer is able to identify in some way with the person carrying out the aggressive acts on the screen (Zillmann 1979; Eron 1982). Modelling not only applies to overt behaviour but also relies on cognitive processes as according to social learning theory it contributes to the formation of concepts, attitudes and needs.

Criticisms of the behavioural model

Behavioural psychotherapy has been subjected to a number of criticisms, some of which relate to its explanation of psychopathology, others to what is identified as abnormal or undesirable behaviour. Some critics, for example, point out that the underlying rationale of behaviour therapy is learning theory, and that most conditioning experiments have been done with animals. It is very doubtful whether all animal learning, let alone human learning, is due to conditioning. Critics such as Yates (1970) point to the limited value of behavioural work for the range of mental health problems referred to psychiatric service.

The other major source of criticism centres on the definition and the implications of the definition of maladaptive behaviour used in behaviourist terminology. Maladaptive behaviour may be generally defined as unsuitable or counterproductive behaviour or behaviour that is inappropriate to the situation. However, this terminology of specific behaviours still does not answer questions regarding what constitutes 'maladaptive', 'unwanted' or 'unacceptable' behaviour, and who makes such judgements. Further, behaviour viewed as acceptable or desirable by one person or group may not be so by others. Generally those who have more power tend to define 'reality'. What constitutes unwanted behaviour is not self-evident but is socially negotiated. As we describe in Chapter 7, acceptable and unacceptable behaviours reflect both the power relationships and the value system operating in a culture at a point of time.

Related to this criticism is another, that the behavioural model conforms with rather than challenges cultural norms. One example was the role taken by behaviour therapists in seeking to convert homosexual men into heterosexuals by using electroshock aversion therapy. Here we also see gender differences. Male problems were referred to more frequently or given more priority. More benign behavioural methods were used for lesbian patients requesting reorientation – such as desensitization and assertiveness training – whereas men were singled out for aversion treatment. The latter not only failed to induce a shift of sexual orientation in gay men; it induced phobic anxiety and impotence in some of its recipients (Diamont 1987). Thus, the behavioural model may be criticized for its role in encouraging conformity to societal norms and not considering wider social and moral issues such as questioning notions of what is considered to be 'maladaptive' in a society at any particular time and the type of treatment deemed appropriate.

Other therapies are subject to similar criticism. Psychoanalysis has also pathologized homosexuality, despite Freud's acceptance of homosexuality as an inversion rather than a perversion. In the nineteenth century the assumed biological determination of homosexuality led not to active physical intervention – as was the case with madness – but with a fatalism that prompted little therapeutic interest (Bullough 1987). However, in the twentieth century psychiatry moved in the same direction as psychoanalysis and behaviourism. Both male and female homosexuality were considered to be pathological and conditions suitable for treatment by psychiatry, because they were generally viewed as problematic.

This particular issue illustrates factors pertinent to all definitions of psychopathology. Perhaps the optimism encouraged by environmental/psychological theories of mental disorder has prompted professionals to intervene in certain behaviours. The apparent effectiveness of behaviour therapy, or at other times of other therapies, may have led to a type of omnipotence in the professionals, which then leads in turn to the danger of them becoming arbiters of what is and is not acceptable behaviour in society. Since society is more concerned with overt behaviour than it is with inner feelings – overt behaviour being not only more obvious as well as observable, but also more likely to be experienced as undesirable by others – it is not surprising that behavioural methods, based upon a theory of the origins of undesirable behaviours, proved popular. For the founding father Watson observable behaviour was the only appropriate subject matter for the relatively new science of psychology because he believed that thoughts and feelings could not be measured objectively.

Behaviour therapy or behaviour modification teaches individuals to replace undesirable behaviours with more acceptable patterns. Although the behavioural model helps explain psychopathology, unlike the psychodynamic model, it is not concerned with uncovering unconscious factors that may be behind the maladaptive behaviour and neither does it try to understand why people behave in a certain way, rather they focus on teaching them to change the behaviour.

Although the behavioural model was a reaction in some ways to psychoanalysis, both the psychodynamic and behavioural models present a deterministic view of human functioning. In the behavioural model, environmental factors are thought to shape our behaviour and our behaviour is the sum of all that we have learned. The deterministic approach to human behaviour advocated by the psychodynamic and behavioural models stands in contrast to the humanistic models that emphasize free will and choice.

Over time many behaviour therapists began to recognize the limitations of the model's explanatory power. Although successful in helping people with anxiety, the behavioural model did not lend itself as well to understanding depression. Cognitive determinants of behaviour began to be introduced, resulting in a synthesis of the two approaches in what is known as the cognitive-behavioural model.

Cognitive therapy

It is debatable whether there is much connection between cognitive therapy and cognitive science, which is the experimental study of inner events and mental processes such as reasoning and memory in psychology. Likewise it does not have much connection with the cognitive philosophies such as phenomenology and existentialism. Rather it has been associated with the reaction against psychoanalysis, and with a pragmatic adaptation of behaviour therapy after the decline of strict behaviourism in the 1970s. Neither Beck nor Ellis, the clinical founders of cognitive therapy, drew upon cognitivism when developing their 'cognitive therapy'. There have been some attempts to make *post hoc* connections between recent academic psychology and therapeutic practice, and some cognitivists (Guidano 1987) have attempted to integrate social constructivist and systemic approaches to their work. One strand of cognitive therapy which is highly theoretically informed is cognitive-analytical therapy (Ryle 1990). However, this too has no relationship with cognitive science, but instead is underpinned by selective insights from psychoanalysis and personal construct theory.

In addition to being a reaction against psychoanalysis the emergence of cognitive-behaviour therapy during the 1970s represents an acknowledgment by behaviour therapists that inner events do matter in clinical practice. It was rooted in the anti-theoretical stance of disillusioned behaviourists (Lazarus 1971) and the recollection by behaviourists that learning theory had since Pavlov always considered 'intervening variables' inside the organism (Hawton et al. 1989). The concession to the inner lives of patients, however, did not mean that cognitive therapy had become an exploratory and biographical model, but rather like its immediate predecessor behaviour therapy, remained scientific and prescriptive. Inner life remains the target, like behaviour itself, of the didactic interventions of experts.

Cognitive therapy is concerned with how aspects of cognition, thinking and reasoning, contribute to psychopathology. It was introduced in the 1950s by Albert Ellis and elaborated and popularized in the 1970s by Aaron Beck.

Beliefs that how we think about ourselves and our world influences our behaviour are longstanding although they were highlighted and formalized as a framework for understanding the aetiology and treatment of distress by Ellis and Beck. For example, the Greek stoic philosopher Epictetus, writing in 1 AD pointed out that we cannot choose our external circumstances but we can always choose how we respond to them. Although events do not hurt us, our views of them can cause us distress:

> Happiness and freedom begin with a clear understanding of one principle: some things are within our control and some things are not. It is only after you have faced up to this fundamental rule and learned to distinguish between what you can and can't control that inner tranquillity and outer effectiveness becomes possible.

Similarly Shakespeare noted the power of thought and as Hamlet said 'there is nothing either good or bad but thinking makes it so' (*Hamlet*, Act 11, Scene ii).

Although there is a great difference between the models of cognitive therapy and the cognitive model in academic psychology, some take the view that the popularity of cognitive therapy was paralleled by a movement within academic psychology towards an adoption of the cognitive model. Researchers began to study human beings as information processors, and studied how psychological problems can result when this process goes wrong. For example, within the cognitive model, the symptoms of schizophrenia are seen as representing faults in the way that information is processed. We are constantly bombarded with information from the external environment and if we are to function appropriately we must selectively attend to the information. A breakdown in a person's ability to selectively attend results in them being overwhelmed by information. It has been suggested that people diagnosed with schizophrenia suffer such a breakdown and that their symptoms reflect the subsequent internal confusion. Their withdrawal into themselves is their way of keeping the bombardment of sensory stimulation to a manageable level. Accordingly, if maladaptive behaviour is the result of the way we process information and perceive ourselves, then researchers point out, there are clear implications for therapy. People can be helped to think and perceive themselves and the world around them differently.

It is possible to identify some general assumptions in cognitive therapy:

- How we perceive and experience our world are active processes that involve both external and introspective data;
- Cognitions represent a synthesis of internal and external stimuli;
- How we appraise a situation is evident in our cognitions (thoughts and visual images);
- These cognitions constitute what may be called consciousness or the phenomenal field, which reflects our configuration of ourselves, our past and future, and what we make of our world;
- Alterations in the content of our underlying cognitive structures affect our affective state and behavioural patterns.

Whereas in behaviour therapy the conceptual focus and model of treatment is that of behaviour – for example people are encouraged to change their behaviour through techniques of desensitization, relaxation and breathing exercises – the focus of cognitive approaches is on thoughts, assumptions and beliefs. Clients are taught to identify and change faulty or maladaptive thinking patterns rather than behaviour itself in the first instance. For example, a depressed patient may have come to view him/herself as powerless to change in any way. In therapy the client is encouraged to monitor and identify this way of thinking or distorted cognition, understand the connection between thoughts, feelings and behaviour, test the validity of automatic thoughts, substitute more realistic cognitions and learn to identify and challenge the underlying assumptions that brought about their distorted cognitions and to change them.

Ellis and Beck

Ellis's approach was originally known as rational–emotive therapy (RET) but was later renamed rational emotive behaviour therapy (REBT) in recognition that it contained strong behavioural as well as cognitive components. It is based on the belief that a person's past experiences shape their present thinking patterns. According to this model, people form illogical, irrational thinking patterns that become the cause of their present distress and instigate further irrational ideas. Ellis points out that it is not what happens to us that causes psychological problems, but rather how we come to understand these events.

It is, according to Ellis, our beliefs (B) about activating events (A) that determine the consequences (C) – the A-B-C Model. For example, a person with a strong belief that they must excel at everything (B) is likely to become depressed (C) on failing an exam (A). Irrational beliefs lead to what Ellis called a 'must' ideology which places onerous demands on the person. He proposed that maladaptive behaviour is the result of irrational beliefs (Ellis 1962). In 'A Guide to Rational Living' (Ellis and Harper 1961), Ellis outlines ten basic irrational beliefs which trigger maladaptive emotions and behaviours, such as:

1. It is a necessity for an adult to be loved and approved of by almost everyone for virtually everything;
2. A person must be thoroughly competent, adequate and successful in all respects;
4. It is catastrophic when things are not going the way one would like;
8. The past is all-important. Because something once strongly affected someone's life, it should continue indefinitely.

A person who holds a strong belief that they must be liked by everyone (B) is likely to become depressed (C) if someone does not like them (A). In Ellis's REBT model, the therapist tries to help the client modify his or her irrational beliefs and to replace them with new and more rational beliefs such as 'It's not essential that everyone likes me', or 'Some people might like me others might not like me'. The therapy is active, challenging and directive.

Another approach within the cognitive model is that of Aaron Beck. Again, psychological problems result from faulty thinking, and the aim of Beck's cognitive therapy is to change the way in which a person thinks about a situation and to challenge maladaptive ways of thinking. It is these that are thought to contribute to the development and maintenance of psychological problems. Like Ellis, Beck observed that his clients thought patterns showed evidence of irrational thinking that he calls systematic distortions. He highlights how a negative cognitive triad of person's view of self, world and future leads to depression. His typology of cognitive distortions is similar to Ellis's typology of irrational beliefs. It represents evidence of emotion subsuming the logical thought process, that is, they are logical fallacies. Some of the illogical ways of thinking discussed by Beck are:

- Arbitrary inference involves making a judgment without any real sound logic or reason;

● Selective abstraction. This is also referred to as 'selective memory'.

● Overgeneralization is the process of making weak analogies between one event, or a small group of events, and an entire system;

● Magnification/minimization implies weighing an event as too important, or failing to weigh it enough.

In *Depression, Causes and Treatment* (1967), Beck initially presented a model of depression, but it now represents a general model of psychopathology in cognitive therapy. The model emphasizes that emotional disorders are the result of distorted thinking or the unrealistic cognitive appraisal of life events. People begin to formulate rules for living early on in life, magnify their difficulties and failures, minimize their accomplishments and successes, arrive at conclusions based on only a selection of evidence, arrive at conclusions despite the absence of supporting evidence, or arrive at conclusions based on a single and trivial event. He suggests a distinction between 'Primitive thinking' and 'Mature thinking':

Primitive thinking is non-dimensional and global: 'I am the living embodiment of failure.'
Mature thinking is multidimensional and specific: 'I make mistakes sometimes, but otherwise I can be clever at many things.'

Primitive thinking is absolutistic and moralistic: 'I am a sinner, and I will end up in hell.'
Mature thinking is relativistic and non-judgmental: 'I sometimes let people down, but there is no reason I can't make amends.'

Primitive thinking is invariant: 'I am hopeless.'
Mature thinking is variable: 'There may be some way.'

Primitive thinking enters into 'character diagnosis': 'I am a coward.'
Mature thinking examines behaviours – behaviour diagnosis: 'I am behaving like a coward right now.'

Primitive thinking is irreversible and sees things as immutable: 'There is just nothing I can do about this.'
Mature thinking is reversible, flexible and ameliorative: 'Let's see what I can do to fix this.'

According to cognitive models, cognitive dysfunctions are the core of the affective, physical and other associated features of depression. Beck argues that illogical ways of thinking lead to a negative view of the self, of current experience and of the future. These negative views make up what Beck terms a negative cognitive triad underlying depression. The negative cognitive triad is experienced by people as negative automatic thoughts, characterized by pessimistic ways of thinking. Apathy and low energy are results of a person's expectation of failure in all areas of his or her life. They learn self-defeating cognitive styles, to expect failure and punishment, and for this to continue for a long time.

The goal of cognitive therapy is to identify and test negative cognitions, to develop alternative and more flexible schemas, and to rehearse both new cognitive and behavioural responses. There is a reciprocal relationship between affect and cognition: one reinforces the other, resulting in escalations of emotional and cognitive impairment. Cognitions – verbal or pictorial representations, available to the conscious, based on assumptions – are termed schemas. Cognitive schemas are in turn presuppositions that organize and filter incoming data, based on past experience, on how to interpret the world. These cognitive schemas develop early in life. When we are infants we take in as much data as possible. Eventually, we deal with this endless stream of data with cognitive filters, schemas, or a set of assumptions and expectations of how events will transpire, and what they mean to us. Cognitive distortions that are too dissonant lead to maladjustment.

In the model of cognitive therapy every psychopathological disorder has its own specific cognitive profile of distorted thought. For example:

- Depressive disorder: global, negative view of self, present experience and expectations for future;
- Hypomanic episode: inflated view of self, present experience and future expectations;
- Anxiety disorder: the fear of physical or psychological danger;
- Panic disorder: catastrophic misinterpretation of body and mental experiences;
- Phobia: danger in specific, avoidable situations;
- Paranoid personality disorder: negative bias, interference by others;
- Obsessive-compulsive disorder: repeated warning or doubting about safety and repetitive rituals to ward off these threats;
- Suicidal behaviour: hopelessness and deficit in problem solving;
- Anorexia nervosa: fear of being fat;
- Hypochondriasis: attribution of serious medical disorder.

Beck's cognitive therapy is now a well-established, effective treatment for depression (Dobson 1989; Hollon and Beck 1994). Beck's cognitive approach has also been applied to understanding a wide range

of psychological problems, for example, anxiety disorders (Beck and Emery 1985) and personality disorders (Beck and Freeman 1990).
There is growing evidence for the effectiveness of the cognitive approach for different forms of psychopathology, although one of the criticisms of Ellis's REBT is that there has been less systematic investigation of its effectiveness with different forms of psychopathology. In the long term, evidence suggests that cognitive therapies are more effective than drug therapies (Evans et al. 1992). However, many therapists take a pragmatic view that no one model of psychopathology can give a full understanding of how psychopathology develops or how it should be treated. Thus many theorists have become interested in finding ways in which different models can be integrated. The best-known integration of models is the cognitive-behavioural model.

The cognitive-behavioural model

Cognitive-behavioural therapy (CBT) may be described as an umbrella model encompassing different aspects of both the cognitive and behavioural models. The underlying assumption is that changing relevant thoughts, beliefs and faulty learning patterns leads to an improvement in mood. It is an action-oriented therapy that assumes that thinking patterns cause maladaptive behaviour and 'negative' emotions. Maladaptive behaviour is behaviour that is counter-productive, or interferes with everyday living. CBT claims that changing the way a person thinks and behaves can have a profound effect on their emotional state. The goal of therapy is of promoting change by helping alleviate symptoms of psychopathology and by addressing a myriad of psychosocial behavioural issues.

One of the first CBT techniques was self instructional training developed by Donald Meichenbaum (1977), which focuses on how thought processes affect behaviour. He was interested in how what people say to themselves both internally and externally influences their behaviour. Meichenbaum pays attention to internal dialogues and during therapy the client is encouraged to externalize his or her dialogues and then to change the instructions that they give to themselves. The aim is to increase the use of adaptive self-talk and decrease dysfunctional self-talk.

Cognitive schemas, developed early in life, determine patterns of behaviour. These schemas are a set of assumptions and beliefs that act as a perceptual filter. These cognitive schemas often include dysfunctional, irrational beliefs that cause people to think and behave in negative ways. Negative thinking and behaviour can result in psychological problems such as depression and anxiety disorders. According to the CBT model, the cause of negative feelings such as sadness, fear and inappropriate guilt is dysfunctional thinking and behaviour and thus it seeks to change maladaptive schemas.

Understanding the issues that lie behind presenting problems or symptoms of psychopathology may be illustrated in the following example. A patient suffering from depression avoids social contact with others, thereby suffering further emotional distress because of his/her isolation. When questioned why s/he avoids others, the patient reveals a fear of rejection. Further exploration in therapy reveals that the patient does not fear rejection as such but rather holds the belief that s/he is boring and unlovable. This belief is then challenged, for example by requesting that the patient name friends who care about him/her and enjoy being with him/her. This demonstrates to the client the irrationality of the belief and facilitates new thinking which will change the old behaviour patterns. In this case the person may learn to think 'People do care for me and find me interesting, so I should not have problems meeting new people who may also like me'. If enough 'irrational' cognitions are identified and changed the patient may experience considerable relief from his/her depression. However, this example illustrates that there is little interest in *why* the patient initially feels uninteresting and unlovable. This is assumed to be a fundamental belief which therapy seeks to challenge.

Although the behavioural and cognitive models have often been treated as separate models of psychopathology, the distinction is not clear-cut in practice. CBT covers a wide range of approaches, some of which are more behavioural and some of which are more cognitive in their emphasis. The cognitive behavioural approach has however become a dominant perspective in psychology as well as a popular approach in self-help literature (Persaud 1998; Davies 2002).

More research has been carried out on cognitive-behavioural therapy than on any other therapy based on psychological models (Roth and Fonagy 1996). For example, CBT approaches are well established as a way of treating panic disorders (Barlow et al. 1989), insomnia and sleep problems (Davies 1999), generalized anxiety disorders (Chambless and Gillis 1993), obsessive-compulsive disorders (Salkovskis and Kirk 1997), with people suffering from psychosis (Fowler et al. 1995), and for a range of physical health problems such as chronic pain (Keefe et al. 1992).

In the development of the cognitive-behavioural model psychologists have adopted the language of psychiatrists, that is, the use of diagnostic terms and classification systems such as found in *The Diagnostic and Statistical Manual of Mental Disorders*. They have tested the techniques of cognitive behavioural therapy in relation to the various categories of disorders delineated in these systems. Although psychologists' adoption of the medical model has been important in gaining legitimization for those psychological therapies within the medical profession and health service, this, perhaps, has been at some cost (Albee 2000).

There are some general commonalities between the bio-medical and the less exploratory psychological models of psychopathology, such as cognitive-behavioural therapy. Both take an interest in what the patient is saying – as indeed do the psychoanalytic and humanistic models. However, although in slightly different ways, the bio-medical and CBT models both treat what is said as information with which to build up an expert formulation. The psychiatrist relies wholly on symptoms – what patients say – in order to make a decision about a diagnosis and to prescribe a treatment. The cognitive therapist builds up a picture of the patient's cognitions and a functional understanding of their role in their life. It is at this point that some, such as Bannister (1983) draw our attention to the similarities between the cognitive and the more exploratory versions of psychological therapy in the therapeutic process of change, when the point is reached that leads the patient to reconstrue some aspect of his/her life. Further, Bannister (1983) and Ryle (1990) point out that even behavioural techniques such as systematic desensitization are simply one amongst many ways in which people come to a reconstruction. If a distinction can be made between the more prescriptive approaches in psychiatry and clinical psychology, and the exploratory psychotherapies it is that in the latter the broader autobiographical content and the shifting meanings negotiated in the relationship are more complex and open-ended.

Criticisms of cognitive-behavioural approaches

Although generally research evidence is taken as supporting the effectiveness of cognitive-behavioural approaches to therapy, there have been critics of this approach. Some question the extent to which the research findings can be generalized to routine clinical settings (White 2000).

Another line of criticism emanating from the socio-cultural model of psychopathology focuses on the adequacy of CBT itself as a model of psychopathology. For example, Smail views the underlying ideas behind cognitive-behavioural approaches as an

> extraordinarily simplistic collection of ideas about how people come to be the way they are and what they can be expected to be able to do about it. Such ideas, acceptable enough to undergraduate students learning the experimental ropes, ring particularly hollow when they come to be applied in the clinical setting, where people's difficulties are often complicated and intractable. (1996: 29–30)

Many psychodynamic and humanistic therapists would agree. Other critics point out that behaviour therapies have traditionally neglected the social setting and context in which therapy takes place and the relationship that develops between the therapist and the client. Although many cognitive-behavioural therapists have begun to recognize the importance of the therapeutic relationship and to question the assumption that the therapist is mechanistic (Schaap et al. 1993), it is still open to question whether this also influences views about the part *other* relationships play in symptoms.

There have also been criticisms of the cognitive model from behaviourists. Skinner (1990) argues that the cognitive model is a return to unscientific mentalism in its speculation about phenomena that are not amenable to measurement or observation, and are outside the domain of scientific enquiry. However, despite his reservations, most theorists agree that such speculation is useful, although there remains disagreement about the nature of those internal processes, as seen in the different views held by the cognitive and psychoanalytical models.

The criticism that these models of psychopathology represent an overly simplistic approach to understanding human problems, and that the therapies derived from these models lack any real recognition of the importance of the therapeutic relationship is one particularly made by humanistic models of therapy, and it is this model which is addressed in the next chapter.

CHAPTER 6

Humanistic models

Humanistic models partly developed as a reaction against what appeared to be the determinism implicit in psychoanalysis and behaviourism. In psychoanalysis, especially if understood from a Freudian perspective before object relations theory, there was a rather pessimistic view of human nature that portrayed people as basically driven by sexual and aggressive impulses that have to be contained. Behaviourism was also seen as objectifying and dehumanizing, emphasizing environmental forces as determinants of behaviour. In contrast, the humanistic approach was to emphasize human nature as essentially positive, valued choice, values and purpose in life; and psychopathology is seen as the failure to fulfil the natural potential for personal growth.

The humanistic model encompasses a wide and diverse range of approaches. While in this chapter we include different examples within this model, in particular we focus on the approach of Carl Rogers, credited as one of the principal founders of the humanistic school. His work remains significantly influential both in its theoretical approach and in its practical therapeutic strategies and applications. Furthermore, his general approach has inspired other developments aimed at enlarging the understanding and management of psychopathology.

Carl Rogers and person-centred therapy

Rogers (1902–87) is perhaps the most well-known humanistic psychologist and is sometimes credited with being the founder of contemporary counselling. His approach to psychopathology developed as an alternative approach to the psychoanalytical, behavioural and medical models prevalent at the time of his own training. Kirschenbaum (1979) and Thorne (1992) both outline Rogers' career and professional development. He was deeply opposed to the bio-medical model of psychopathology, both in its theoretical conceptualizations concerning the genesis of distress and in the practical intervention it viewed as appropriate to alleviate the manifestations of distress. He was sceptical about the use of psychometric tests if their main purpose was simply to diagnose and label either problems or people. Rogers' person-centred therapy emphasizes the capacity in clients to find their own answers, once the necessary psychological conditions had been established. He applied his ideas derived from therapy to wider contexts, such as education, conflict resolution and encounter groups (see Thorne 1992).

The essence of Rogers' approach to psychopathology is based on his view that there is an inherent human motive for self-growth, or what he terms self-actualization, present in all people. In the right conditions a child increasingly develops positive self-regard and the actualizing tendency is promoted. However, during the course of development this striving can become frustrated, blocked or distorted, when the person receives *conditional* positive regard from his or her social environment, and thus develops what Rogers referred to as conditional positive self-regard. For example, if someone grows up in an environment where he or she learns from significant adults the belief that one has to please others in order to be loved and valued, he or she can only find value for themselves to the extent that they live up to this belief. Psychopathology is the result of the tension between a person's inner actualizing tendency, and the conditional positive regard they receive from others. The distress resulting from manifestations of psychopathology can be ameliorated through the experience of positive relationships where the person is given unconditional positive regard. Through this experience, the person increasingly develops positive self-regard, the actualizing tendency is promoted and dysfunctional behaviour on the part of the client decreases. Thus, the person-centred model is holistic, viewing and addressing the entire experience of being a person in its consideration of human distress, rather than selecting specific symptoms of psychopathology as the focus of concern.

The actualizing tendency

The cornerstone of Rogers' theory, the actualizing tendency, is a motivational force directed towards constructive growth. 'It is the urge which is evident in all organic and human life – to expand, extend, to become autonomous, develop, mature – the tendency to express and activate all the capacities of the organism, to the extent that such activation enhances the organism or the self' (Rogers 1961: 35). The fully functioning person is one who is:

> synonymous with optimal psychological adjustment, optimal psychological maturity, complete congruence, complete openness to experience . . . since some of these terms sound somewhat static, as though such a person 'had arrived', it should be pointed out that all the characteristics of such a person are process characteristics. The fully functioning person would be a person – in-process, a person continually changing. (1959: 235)

In humanistic therapy, it is the therapist's trust in this actualizing tendency that makes it so radically different from other therapeutic approaches (see Bozarth 1998). The person-centred therapist attempts to stand shoulder to shoulder with and become a companion to the client in their explorations towards self understanding. Rogers (1957) describes how in his experience he found that whatever troubled people, whether distressing feelings or difficult interpersonal relationships, they were all struggling with the same existential question, of how to be themselves.

Rogers (1957) states that for constructive personality change to occur then six conditions are necessary in the therapy. They also appear to suggest what a healthy way of being is, as opposed to inhibiting factors to personal growth. The conditions include being in psychological contact with another (or others), being congruent and genuine, being vulnerable or anxious, having unconditional positive regard, and being empathic and unconditionally accepting. The therapeutic relationship is characterized as one that tries to maintain these conditions at a heightened level of intensity.

The person-centred therapist does not attempt to change the client in any specific way, that is, its goal is not to address specific manifestations of psychopathology. For example the therapist does not set out to cure the client's depression or alleviate their anxiety. The therapist is not so much concerned with the reasons for a client's feelings but rather with how they feel. Exploring these ideas in the 1960s, Rogers studied the impact of his approach in research with hospitalized schizophrenics. As researchers in the person-centred tradition do not generally adopt the medical model, research data on person-centred therapy for specific psychiatric disorders is generally lacking. However some studies, such as Greenberg and Watson (1998), show that humanistic person-centred therapies are effective for the alleviation of various forms of distress such as depression. Despite the general lack of research most take the view that person-centred therapy is less effective for severe and chronic conditions, although recent writers have begun to explore its use with psychosis and personality disorders (Lambers 1994).

There have been a number of criticisms of the person-centred approach. Rogers has been criticized as presenting an overly optimistic view of human nature. Some have questioned how can there be so much suffering in the world if people are basically trustworthy, social and constructive in nature. In response to such criticisms, Rogers states:

> I am certainly not blind to all the evil and the terribly irresponsible violence that is going on . . . There are times that I think I don't give enough emphasis on the shadowy side of our nature, the evil side. Then I start to deal with a client and discover how, when I get to the core, there is a wish for more socialization, more harmony, more positive values. Yes, there are all kinds of evil abounding in the world but I do not believe this in inherent in the human species any more than I believe that animals are evil. (Zeig 1987: 202)

Another line of criticism comes from adherents of the socio-cultural model of psychopathology who point out that Rogers' approach does not in any real sense explore the client's wider social context. They point to the influence on Rogers and contemporary humanistic writers such as George Kelly, of their own social context, which shaped their perspectives on human nature. The possibility of individual change, personal responsibility and personal freedom all reflect the individualism of American ideology. It may also be questioned whether such ideas as responsibility, choice and capacity for change are really something in an individual's control, that can be changed at will.

Some writers have criticized as simplistic Rogers' view that psychopathology develops through the internalization of conditions of worth.

> Rogers' simplistic explanation of the genesis of people's problems has led to a unitary diagnosis: namely that of being out of touch

with the valuing process inherent in the actualising tendency. Consequently, he has restricted himself to what is essentially a single treatment approach. This is an inadequate way to approach the range of difficulties that people have in being personally responsible. (Nelson-Jones 1982: 25–6)

Against this, others question the assumption that there are specific treatments for specific problems, arguing that the evidence is insufficient to draw such a conclusion (Bozarth 1998). Another criticism concerns the concept of the actualizing tendency. Some have called this concept naive (Ellis 1959). Similar to other abstract psychological concepts that cannot be directly observed, such as Freud's concepts of id, ego and superego, it is impossible to ascertain whether an actualizing tendency actually exists. Others, although accepting the general principle, have viewed it as an insufficient basis on which to build a theoretical framework and approach to therapy, and see a need for therapists to introduce other, cognitive and behavioural techniques to bring about effective therapeutic change (Nelson-Jones 1984). Other criticisms point out that the imprecise language and vagueness of concepts make it difficult for concepts to be subjected to empirical testing (Coffer and Appley 1964).

Personal construct psychology

The belief in the ability of individuals to develop and grow in a positive direction is the core theme throughout all humanistic approaches. One that also developed in the USA in the 1950s and gained a significant following in Britain is George Kelly's personal construct psychology.

Bannister, one of the main proponents of personal construct psychology in Britain, describes his own resistance to psychoanalysis and to learning theory based behaviourism in an article on personal construct psychology, titled 'A new theory of personality' (1966):

All psychological theories seem to imply some sort of model man, some notion of what man essentially is. Thus psychoanalytic theories suggest that man is essentially a battlefield, he is a dark cellar in which a maiden aunt and a sex-crazed monkey are locked in mortal combat, the affair being refereed by a rather nervous bank clerk. Alternatively, learning theory and stimulus-response psychology generally seem to suggest that man is essentially a ping-pong ball with a memory. (Bannister 1966: 363)

Fundamental to the personal construct approach is that through our experience and interaction with others, we form constructs about others and ourselves. Even though Kelly is opposed to the empirical model of behaviourism, he describes what he calls a model of man in terms of man being like a scientist. By this Kelly means that we form a hypothesis about an event based on our past experiences of that event. We test out that hypothesis which is then either confirmed or disproved. Our hypotheses are modified accordingly. For Kelly, psychopathology is based on the form and content of our personal construct systems. Construct systems are set up through the constellation of constructs that are subject to continuous revision. These construct systems are determined by our past experience of events and influence what we perceive and how we perceive. This information undergoes a process of filtering and transformation in our construct system, modifying the way we construe experiences, influencing our expectations and guiding our behaviour. For example, if our experiences have led us to construe the world as a dangerous place we will be fearful or anxious. Likewise if we have not previously encountered a particular situation, it will be outside the range of convenience of our construct system and we will feel anxious. Distress can be ameliorated in personal construct psychology through the therapist exploring with the client his/her personal construct system.

Bannister and his colleagues carried out pioneering research work applying personal construct theory to psychopathology (Bannister 1960, 1965; Bannister and Fransella 1965; Bannister and Salmon 1966). Bannister, for example, explored the conceptual structures in people diagnosed as thought disordered schizophrenics. Using the repertory grid technique derived from personal construct theory it was found that schizophrenic thought patterns showed evidence of construct systems that are either too loose or too tight (too diffuse or too specific thought patterns). For example, if during the process of development, one's predictions of events are continually invalidated by experience, this will render prediction of future events uncertain. Thus a loose construing process is established to encompass information to deal with a vast array of possible eventualities. The result is that irrelevant data is not rejected or filtered and the person is overwhelmed with information. In such a case constructs will be too loose to offer any explanatory framework or to be of use in organizing experience and in predicting and guiding behaviour. Too tight construing leads to an inflexible framework that does not accommodate the necessary information needed for effective construing of the world.

Transactional analysis

Another humanistic-existential therapy which contributes its own understanding of psychopathology is transactional analysis, founded by Eric Berne (1910–70), who initially trained as a psychoanalyst (Berne 1971). The practice of transactional analysis (TA) is founded on three assumptions common to the humanistic approaches (Stewart 1989). The first assumption is that at their core, people are 'OK'. Although the therapist may not like the person's behaviour, the therapist values and esteems the client. The second is that the therapist holds that each person has the capacity to think and make decisions about their life. The third assumption is that people can behave differently, so that the way they think, feel and behave is their own choice.

Berne outlines a complex theoretical framework that therapists use to discuss with clients the nature of interpersonal communication. He suggests a model that is made up of three ego states – the child, the parent and the adult state. In the child ego state, Berne describes how we think and feel in the way that we did when we were children. In the parent ego state we think and feel in a similar way to those of the significant parental figures of our childhood. In our adult ego state we think and feel in ways that are direct responses to the here and now environment. Any behaviour is driven by the ego state that is in control of the personality at that moment. For example, feelings such as those of inferiority or feelings of spontaneous happiness and joy are associated with the child. Criticism and orthodoxy are associated with the parent. Objective, unemotional appraisal of the environment is associated with the adult. Typically we move in and out of these different ego states. In this approach psychopathology can be viewed as being due to the breakdown of barriers between ego states. For example, delusional ideation occurs where there is a breakdown between child and adult ego states so that child imagery contaminates the adult appraisal of the world.

Interpersonal interactions are analysed in terms of the communication between individuals at an ego state level. For example, at a social level it might appear that we are talking adult to adult, but at the psychological level something else may be happening, such as parent talking to child, or child to parent. Berne also describes the pathological games that people play in terms of stereotyped ego state communication. TA in fact provides an elaborate framework of psychopathology, with the view similar to psychoanalytic thinking, that psychological problems often have their roots in childhood. Berne similarly describes how each individual has a life script. This is the plan decided in early life by each person about the course of their life, how it begins, what happens in the middle and how it ends. The life script is laid down between 3 and 7 years of age and reflects one of four possible judgements about the self and others!

- I'm OK and you're OK;
- I'm not OK, but you're OK;
- I'm OK, but you're not OK;
- I'm not OK, and you're not OK.

These judgements originate from parental messages that the child acquires at such a young age that they are not the product of reasoned and logical thinking. However, they form the basis of the way the child experiences his or her life. The life script represents the infant's way of surviving and getting their needs met in what seems to be a hostile world, but the choice of life script is not made at the conscious level. Berne describes how the life script is like each person's own unfolding drama. These life scripts are carried into adulthood and played out unconsciously, usually confirming early decisions. Although each person has their own unique life script, Berne describes some typical scripts: 'I mustn't grow up; I mustn't be important; I mustn't exist; I mustn't make it; I mustn't feel; I mustn't be me' (1964).

The therapist aims to facilitate the client's recognition that he or she can now make different decisions (see Stewart 1989). The person is then acting as an autonomous human being rather than a being at the mercy of a predetermined life script.

Existential approaches

One of the influences on Rogers was his interest in existential philosophy (Thorne 1992). He often refers to the writings of two philosophers in particular, whose ideas resonate with his approach: Buber and Kierkegaard. In some aspects, the person-centred approach, TA and Gestalt therapy may be thought of as forms of humanistic-existential philosophy (Rogers 1973). However, the work most associated with the humanistic-existential approach is that of Victor Frankl (1905–97). Frankl's experiences during the Second World War when he spent three years in the Nazi concentration camps, during which time he suffered the deaths of his parents, wife and brother, led him to explore issues about the search for meaning. He came to believe that a fundamental purpose in life is to find meaning in a world that seems meaningless (1963, 1967). People find meaning in their lives, for example, through achievement, transcendent experience, or through suffering. Frankl developed a system of therapy known as logotherapy in which clients are helped to become fully aware of their own responsibilities, to develop choices over what attitudes and beliefs they hold, and to face the existential void of life. The therapeutic aim is to raise the person's consciousness. Other existential therapists include Ludwig Binswanger (1881–1966) and Medard Boss (1903–2001) who similarly seek to understand the meaning of personal experience, using philosophy rather than psychology to understand the human predicament.

Transpersonal psychotherapy

The main themes of existential psychotherapy, include questions around the meaning and purpose of life, issues of good and evil, life and death, overlap to some extent with transpersonal psychotherapy (Rowan 1993). Rogers too, towards the end of his life, became interested in altered states of consciousness and began to advocate a more spiritual understanding of human experience. He was interested in the views of Arthur Koestler who believed that individual consciousness was but a fragment of cosmic consciousness (Rogers 1980). Rogers wrote about the times when he felt most effective as a therapist: 'At those moments it seems that my inner spirit has reached out and roughed the inner spirit of the other. Our relationship transcends itself and becomes part of something larger. Profound growth and healing and energy are present' (1980: 129).

Some writers have discussed spirituality within the person-centred approach (Thorne 1994; Purton 1998). Generally, humanistic-existential approaches are more readily integrated with spiritual ideas than other models, for example, the cognitive and behavioural models (see Payne et al. 1992) although some within the psychoanalytical model, notably Jung, addressed these issues. Transpersonal psychology and psychotherapy engages with experiences that transcend or go beyond the realms of ordinary human consciousness and experience. Abraham Maslow is credited with being the founder of the transpersonal approach, and leading figures include Grof and Wilber in the United States and Rowan in Britain, all of whom question the narrow perceptions of reality recognized by most psychological theories.

In Maslow's model the basic characteristic of human beings is again their striving to fulfil their self-potential. However, whereas Rogers viewed behaviour as being driven by the self-concept, Maslow was concerned with the *motives* that drive people. He describes two basic kinds of motivations. The first he terms the deficiency motivation, which is the need to reduce physiological tensions such as hunger and thirst. The second he describes as the growth motivation, which is due to the satisfaction of needs such as the need to be loved and the need to be esteemed. In Maslow's approach, human needs are organized hierarchically in what he terms 'a hierarchy of needs'. The basic human needs for survival first have to be met, so that physiological needs such as food, drink and sex are satisfied. When these needs have been met the next set of needs concern safety and security, and include psychological security and being out of danger. The next set of needs in the hierarchy are concerned with love and belonging, including needs to affiliate with and be accepted by others. The last stage is reached when all other needs have been met, and the individual strives to meet their needs for self-actualization. Achieving self-actualization is not an all or nothing process. It comes about over time by means of small changes. According to Maslow, self-actualized individuals are self-directed, creative, independent, have an accurate self view and accurate view of others, are willing to try and understand other people's points of view, and are open to new experiences. Maslow's concept of the ideal self-actualized person is very similar to Carl Rogers' view of the ideal fully functioning person.

Maslow describes self-actualized people as those who are open to experience. One form that particularly interests him is what he describes as peak experiences. These transcend ordinary human consciousness and are often experienced as religious or spiritual in nature.

Others have gone on to develop transpersonal psychology and have tried to integrate their ideas with those of Jung. Stanislav Grof (Grof and Bennett 1990) integrates Jung's ideas in his study of the spiritual aspects of consciousness. He arrived at many of his conclusions after observing people in altered states of consciousness. One aspect of his approach that is similar to the more traditional humanistic approaches is the emphasis on the therapist accepting and trusting the spontaneous unfolding of human experience. This also has a similarity with Jung's theory that there is an inner wisdom for healing which comes from the collective unconscious. From the perspective of transpersonal psychology, experiences that psychiatrists may diagnose as indicating mental illnesses can be conceptualized in a different way, as part of a framework of spiritual or peak experiences. Some adherents of the humanistic and transpersonal schools doubt the value of traditional scientific enquiry. Instead they draw on quantum physics to provide a theoretical foundation for their work. For example Tart (1975) puts forward the view that there are realms of awareness beyond those that are understandable to us at present. He argues that we perceive only a small segment of reality. Our consensus reality is merely the one that we have agreed upon as real and important. He points out that traditional science can only confirm that our perceptions are realistic in a particular cultural framework, that is that we agree with each other on those specific items that we have selected from our conscious reality. Others within the transpersonal approach have focused on the relationship between Western psychotherapy and the ideas of Eastern religious traditions. Eastern thought emphasizes the interconnectedness of all things and how it is an illusion to see ourselves as separate from the world around us. A key figure here is Ken Wilber (1998), who like Jung has attempted to integrate the religious traditions of the East with the psychology of the West.

The humanistic model and the medical model

In this chapter we have condensed some of the humanistic therapies in a way that does less than justice to them, were it not that the concept of psychopathology is one that they generally do not favour. Transactional analysis is perhaps the only humanistic model that really employs a set of concepts referring to psychopathology. Otherwise, psychopathology in the humanistic models is viewed as the result of the actualizing tendency being thwarted in some way. Psychopathology is addressed through the therapeutic relationship between therapist and client where the task of the client-centred therapist is to create a facilitative environment that nurtures the actualizing tendency. The humanistic model has also not generally adopted the language of psychiatry, such as DSM-IV. This may be one reason why humanistic therapy has not gained the same credibility within the psychiatric and medical profession as cognitive and behavioural models.

Although the cognitive and behavioural models of psycho-pathology do not assume a biological basis for abnormal psycho-logical conditions, they adopt the general paradigm of the medical model. For example they delineate the parameter of understanding as being concerned with specific behaviour or specific conditions. Thus therapists working in the cognitive and behavioural models attempt to define the problem, and administer what has been evaluated the most effective forms of therapy for specific conditions as defined in DSM. By contrast, adherents of the humanistic school such as Rogers and Maslow are generally critical of the underlying premises concerning the aetiology and development of psychopathology in the medical model. They are also critical of the medical model's response to or treatment of psychopathology. For example, Maslow comments on the use of words such as 'patient' in the context of psychotherapy:

> I hate the medical model that they imply because the medical model suggests that the person who comes to the counsellor is a sick person, beset by disease and illness, seeking a cure. Actually, of course, we hope that the counsellor will be the one who helps to foster the self-actualisation of people, rather than the one who helps to cure a disease. (1993: 49)

A major premise of the humanistic model is that judgements of what constitutes 'normal' or 'abnormal' are highly subjective and depend-ent on the clinician's own frame of reference. The role of the therapist in the humanistic model is that of allowing the client both to be and to become, to encourage the person to develop and grow in his or her own way in a process of self-discovery. As we have described, in this respect it differs markedly from the medical model with its emphasis on categorization and diagnostic systems. It also is very different from cognitive and behavioural models in its emphasis on personal responsibility and choice. Humanistic psychology is of course very influential in the field of counselling and psychotherapy, and there is growing interest in transpersonal and existential therapies.

We have already referred to one of the criticisms of the humanistic therapies, to the extent that they do consider issues relating to psychopathology, which is that they reflect the cultural context within which they were formulated and developed (New World opti-mism) as well as being less than adequate in their recognition of cul-tural determinants in the lives of clients. This criticism also extends to other therapies, and it is this sociological dimension that we address in the next chapter.

C H A P T E R 7

Sociological models

Sociological studies point to a social pattern of psychopathology. Although anyone, whatever their social background, can experience varieties of fear, sadness or madness, this does not mean that these states occur randomly. Research findings mainly based upon epidemiological data indicate that social class and poverty (Bromley 1983, 1994) influence physical and mental health, as well as gender (Ussher 1991), sexual orientation (Rothblum 1990), race (Pillay 1993), and age. People in these groups are particularly vulnerable to distress, and are more likely to receive biological or physical treatments and much less likely to receive psychotherapy. When they do they tend to drop out earlier and more frequently (Yamamoto et al. 1968). The one issue that these disparate groups have in common is that they are members of groups differing in some aspect from the dominant culture. They are further disadvantaged by institutions including health systems, which have been developed and are largely organized to meet the needs and requirements of those groups that reflect the power structure of society generally (Clarke and Brindley 1993).

The sociological model contains three main perspectives on psychopathology. These are social causation, labelling theory/social constructivism and critical theory. (For a full review of sociological perspectives, see Pilgrim 1997, and Pilgrim and Rogers 1999.) Within the literature on psychopathology, studies are frequently influenced by versions of more than one perspective (Bury 1986).

Critical theory

During the twentieth century a number of attempts were made to account for the relationship between socio-economic structures and the inner lives of individuals. One example is Sartre when he developed his 'progressive-regressive method' (1963). This was an attempt to understand biography in relation to its social context and understand the social context via the accounts of people's lives. This existential development of humanistic Marxism competed with another set of discussions about the relationship between unconscious mental life and societal determinants and constraints. Within Freud's early circle, a number of analysts took an interest in using their psychological insights in order to illuminate societal processes, which set a trend for later analysts. Out of this tradition emerged a group of Freudian-Marxists, known as 'critical theorists', many of whom were associated with the Frankfurt School, which largely relocated to the States with the rise of Nazism. The difference between this work and most clinical psychoanalysis was the focus on the interrelationship between psyche and society. Horkheimer outlined the question behind its aims:

> What connections can be established, in a specific social group, in a specific period in time, in specific countries, between the group, the changes in the psychic structures of its individual members and the thought and institutions that are a product of that society, and that have, as a whole, a formative effect upon the group under consideration? (1931: 14)

The interrelationship between the material environment of individuals and their cultural life and inner lives was subsequently explored by a number of writers in this group including Marcuse, Adorno, Fromm and Reich – the latter a Marxist psychoanalyst. Within this school, Freudianism was viewed as the legitimate form of psychology that was potentially philosophically compatible with Marxism, although their integration of Freud's views was selective.

The role of this group seems paradoxical. For a theory that drew heavily if selectively upon clinical psychoanalysis, their work focused not on mental illness but on what Fromm called the 'pathology of normalcy'. Psychoanalysis is concerned with the notion that we are all ill, with psychopathology varying between individuals only in degree and type. Accordingly, the concerns of this group were about life negating cultural norms associated with authoritarianism and the capitalist economy and the ambiguous role of the superego as a source of conformity and mutuality. These norms were mediated by intrapsychic mechanisms – especially repression highlighted in Freud's theory of a dynamic unconscious.

Critical theory is evident in studies of the authoritarian personality (Adorno et al. 1950) and the mass psychology of fascism (Reich 1933; Fromm 1942). Aspects of critical theory can be found in a variety of studies that continue to explore the relationship between economics, culture and the psychopathology of the individual (Jacoby 1975; Holland 1978; Lasch 1978; Richards 1984; Kovel 1988; see also the 'anti-psychiatry' writings of Cooper 1968 and Laing 1967). There is a continuing body of work that examines the way in which contemporary western society is developing in a pathological direction – through the culture of narcissism, or the fragmented self represented in the metaphor of schizophrenia (Harvey 1989). These post-war writers have been part of a theoretical tradition that is still psychoanalytically oriented but reflects changes such as the impact of Klein and later object-relations theorists. Another Freudian-Marxist hybrid can be found in the French intellectual world, especially following the work of Althusser and Lacan (Elliot 1992).

Social class and mental health

Sociologists have long debated the exact definitions of social class, highlighting the conceptual problems relating to social class and economic status and the relationship between the two. There is an overall consensus that there is a relationship between social stratification and advantage and disadvantage within society. Social class is a good predictor of a number of outcomes that shape people's lives including mental and physical health. Poverty and poor mental health are correlated (Breen and Rottman 1955; Pahl 1993). Sociologists have drawn our attention to how behaviour is shaped by the social structure. The French sociologist Emile Durkheim (1858–1917) described the sets of values and norms that guide people's behaviour in society so that they behave according to these norms and values. However, when our own values no longer match those of the society in which we live, then our ties with that society are weakened, resulting in anomie. Durkheim related this loss of social cohesion to feelings of anomie and alienation that were linked to some forms of suicide. His study of suicide is held up as the classic study of social causation:

Durkheim's view that external social reality impinges on human action and shapes human consciousness.

Largely based on psychiatric epidemiological studies, sociologists conclude that social class and mental health are correlated. However, they differ in views on why there is such a relationship. The relationship was first studied systematically in the 1930s, by a group of sociologists called The Chicago School (Faris and Dunham 1939). Over a period of 12 years, they studied psychiatric hospital admission, diagnosis and locality of origin in the city. They found the incidence of schizophrenia to be seven times greater in poor, socially disorganized neighbourhoods than in stable suburbs. This work instigated further studies on psychiatric epidemiology that tend to confirm that there is a positive relationship between low social class and psychopathology (Hollingshed and Redlich 1958; Dohrenwend and Dohrenwend 1977; Brown and Harris 1978; Bebbington et al. 1981; Goldberg and Huxley 1992). Overall, the epidemiological evidence points to over-representation of people diagnosed as schizophrenic in lower-class samples (Tietze et al. 1941; Stein 1957; Goldberg and Morrison 1963). These patients are particularly over-represented at the lower end of the social scale (Dunham 1964).

The advantage of this psychiatric epidemiological perspective is that it provides the type of scientific confidence associated with objectivism and empiricism. There are also disadvantages. They do not question assumptions and concepts inherent in the psychiatric model. Correlative studies do not provide information on causality. Further investigations of large subpopulations do not inform us of the lived experience of mental health problems or the variety of meanings attributed to them by patients and significant others.

In addition to studies concerned with psychiatric epidemiology, studies have been carried out to explore the effect of homelessness and unemployment on mental health. Psychiatric research studies indicate the high prevalence of mental illness in homeless populations, providing estimates of the prevalence of psychiatric illnesses as high as 90 per cent (Bassuk et al. 1984). Generally, such studies focus less on homelessness as a cause of distress or as a social policy failure and more on the personal deficits of the homeless, describing the symptomatology, social functioning and the 'maladaptive behaviour' of homeless people. These studies show how social problems have been individualized and medicalized.

Psychological studies on the effects of unemployment on mental health consistently points to the same conclusions. As Fryer (1993) notes, research carried out in Britain in the 1930s came to the same conclusions as contemporary research, where surveys consistently indicate that groups of unemployed people have poorer mental health than groups of comparable employed people. Zadik (1993) points out, vulnerability to ill health often coincides with the threat of redundancy rather than with the exact time that redundancy actually begins. A series of studies carried out in the 1970s and 1980s in Britain on the mental health effects of unemployment (Warr et al. 1988) indicate the psychological effects of unemployment. Experiences of unemployment and economic hardship have been found to be associated with suicide attempts (Ahlburg and Shapiro 1983), while Burchell (1994) and Lampard (1994) indicate that psychological and physical stresses are a result of being made unemployed, rather than predisposing factors towards unemployment.

The mental health of significant others in the life of the unemployed person is also affected. For example, the school performance of children and their mental health is significantly affected by parental unemployment (see reviews by Davies 1995; Fryer 1995). A study by Lampard (1994), demonstrates that unemployment directly increases the risk of marriage break-up. Reviews by Davies (1995) and Fryer (1995) of the empirical evidence regarding the effect on unemployment on mental health, also indicate direct and indirect causal factors that precipitate poor mental health. These causal factors are similar to those found by Brown and Harris (1978) in their study of depressed women in South London, which we discuss below.

As well as epidemiological studies, the literature on life events also highlights the causal relationship between social class and poor mental health. Although people from all social backgrounds suffer stressful life events such as bereavement, illness, unemployment and divorce, the ratio between such negative events and buffering positive ones is not equally distributed in society. A study by Phillips (1968) found no difference in the reporting of negative events between working- and middle-class respondents. However, middle-class respondents were twice as likely to report positive feelings about life. The relationship between social class and positive protecting experiences is confirmed by Myers (1974, 1975). There is a class gradient in mental health and this is related to direct social stress and the absence of positive buffering experiences.

Many of the issues to do with social inequality revolve around those of economic poverty. Poverty is related to psychopathology (Bruce et al. 1991), and a review of the evidence shows that psychological problems are more prevalent in people in a lower social class (see

Argyle 1994). The direct negative effect of poverty on physical health has an indirect impact on mental health (Blaxter 1990).

Social causation vs. social drift

One methodological difficulty with the studies on social class and mental health is that because other social variables such as race, ethnicity and gender interact with social class it is not easy to separate their effects. However, what the studies consistently point out is that there is a correlation between poverty and mental ill health. What has been in dispute is the direction of causality. The social causation view emphasizes that mental ill health is caused by social stress. As life stress increases with poverty then poor people experience more psychological problems (Gunnell et al. 1995; McLeod and Kessler 1990) and have a higher incidence of mental ill health (Dunham 1957). This approach focuses on tracing the relationship between social disadvantage and mental illness, and was popular in the 1950s when a number of large-scale community surveys of the social causes of mental health problems and of the large psychiatric institutions were undertaken (Pilgrim and Rogers 1994). As the main indicator of disadvantage is low social class and/or poverty, studies investigating this relationship have been a strong current within the study of psychiatric populations. However, the most quoted examples of the social causation studies appeared in the late 1970s and early 1980s (Brown and Harris 1978); and studies in the social causation tradition proliferated in the late 1990s with an explicit government policy agenda designed to tackle the social, economic and environmental causes of mental health problems (*Our Healthier Nation*, DoH, 1988).

The alternative hypothesis is the social drift hypothesis, which is that people become poor because their mental health problems make them less competent and employable suggesting that low socio-economic status is an outcome and not a cause of psychopathology (Williams 1990). Thus, those further up the social scale become incompetent and dysfunctional and will drift downward in their class position. This is consistent with a biological or genetic model concerning determinants of psychopathology. A third hypothesis is the interaction hypothesis (Kohn 1973) suggesting that genetically vulnerable people become ill when placed under stress. Kohn also argues that lower-class people are not socialized to be able to cope with stress.

The two main hypotheses of social causation and social drift reflect different assumptions about the causes of mental ill health in different models of psychopathology. The social drift hypothesis reflects a biogenic view that has a long-standing association with eugenics and biological models of psychopathology. In contrast the social causation view is more associated with the disciplines of psychology and sociology and with environmentalist views as to causation; and as such it forms a major tenet of the socio-cultural model of psychopathology. According to the socio-cultural perspective which we describe in the next chapter, many issues to do with social inequality are crucial in understanding the nature and cause of distress, even though the referral for professional help may just request the alleviation of the signs and symptoms of distress.

Sociologists working within this perspective basically accept schizophrenia or depression as legitimate diagnoses and these diagnoses are thus awarded factual status. One of the difficulties in assessing the hypotheses we describe is the role of psychiatric diagnosis. Many of the studies of the class gradient have concerned the patient group with the most conceptually problematic diagnosis – that of 'schizophrenia'. There have been criticisms of this diagnosis as we discuss in more detail later, both from the social constructivist perspective within the sociological model, and from adherents of the socio-cultural approach within the psychological model of psychopathology. Bannister (1968) points out that schizophrenia is a disjunctive category: that is, two patients with the same diagnosis may share no symptoms in common. One may be deluded and excitable and the other hallucinating and flat in affect. Thus some psychologists and sociologists have rejected the schizophrenia concept (Bentall et al. 1988; Boyle 1990). A second major methodological problem with the diagnosis of what psychiatrists call 'serious mental illness' is that research indicates that there is a class bias in diagnosis. Those diagnosing are middle class whereas those given a diagnosis of schizophrenia are more likely to be lower class. Furthermore, the greater the gap of both class and culture between the labeller and the labelled, the more serious the label that is likely to be ascribed (Wilkinson 1975; Horowitz 1983).

Gender

There is a substantial literature on the topic of women and mental health (Baker-Miller 1971; Chessler 1972; Chamberlain 1988; Dutton-Douglas and Walker 1988; Ussher 1991; Ussher and Nicolson 1992). These studies may be categorized into five main areas: the mental health consequences of women's everyday life; black and ethnic minority women; older women; lesbian women and the topic of abuse and mental health (see review, Williams et al. 1993).

Numerous studies point out that more women than men suffer from depression and anxiety in our society. Reviews of the research (Ussher 1991; Williams et al. 1993) indicate that four times as many women than men present with psychological problems to their GP. Similarly, GP referrals to clinical psychologists reflect the same trend, with on average 28 per cent male to 72 per cent female referrals. Other studies suggest that 30–40 per cent of women in particular demographic groups are depressed at any one time. There are also gender imbalances in the form that treatment takes. Women are more likely than men to be prescribed psychotropic drugs (Ashton 1991) or to receive ECT (Frank 1990) and are less likely to be referred to a specialist mental health worker following psychological diagnosis by their GP (Brown et al. 1988). The mental health needs of women from ethnic minorities (CRE 1992), lesbian women (Rothblum 1990) or older women are often ignored.

The two main explanations for this have been that of biological vulnerability and social causality. These are sometimes seen as alternative and sometimes as additive explanations. The biological vulnerability argument points to physiological reasons why women are more prone to mental distress. These include the post-natal distress of depression and puerperal psychosis, the role of pre-menstrual tension in creating temporary distress or amplifying psychological problems, and the greater prevalence of senile dementia in women. Childbirth is associated with depression, with estimates varying between 10–30 per cent (Nicolson 1989). However, the picture is not so clearcut as to warrant purely physiological explanations.

Within the social causality perspective for this gender imbalance there are two explanations. One refers to the labelling model, suggesting that women are more likely to be labelled as mentally ill. For example, Ussher points out that behaviour viewed as 'acceptable' in men, such as assertion or aggression, is often labelled as a sign of pathology when women exhibit the same behaviour.

The second explanation concerns social vulnerability, suggesting that women's experiences and their role within a patriarchal society predisposes them to depression. There are many aspects of women's lives that act as risk factors for depression, for example, economic vulnerability, lack of power or control and physical and sexual abuse (Ussher 1991). The social causation view is that because women are under greater social stress than men they become mentally ill more often. This view does not necessarily challenge the validity of psychiatric diagnosis. Studies demonstrate the psychological costs for women of daily life in a society structured by gender. Marriage is more likely to be beneficial to the psychological well-being of men, and detrimental to the psychological well-being of women (McRae and Brody 1989). Domestic violence is carried out mainly by men on their female partners (Smith 1989). The links between battering and long-term mental health problems are well established (Rosewater 1985). Caring for children and dependent relatives takes a high toll on mental health when linked with isolation, low social value and a lack of resources (Brown and Harris 1978; Smith 1991). The links between poverty and psychological distress and disturbance are well documented (Bruce et al. 1991). However, poverty and levels of economic deprivation are much higher amongst women than men, with poverty among women being correlated with being a single parent (National Council for One-Parent Families 1987); with being divorced (Day and Bahr 1986); with being old (Bruce et al. 1991); and with being black or a member of an ethnic minority group (EOC 1992).

One of the best known studies developed within a social causation framework is the Camberwell South London study of depressed women called *Social Origins of Depression: a Study of Psychiatric Disorder in Women* (Brown and Harris 1978). Over the past 25 years this original study has been extended to include international comparisons. The study found that women who were diagnosed as depressed were more likely to have young children at home, less employment, and fewer people to talk to about their worries than those women who were not diagnosed as depressed. This landmark study drew attention to the social origins of depression. Brown and Harris's model point to the aetiology of depression as being multi factorial so that some factors may be present and yet the person depresses. It refers to protective as well as vulnerability factors, past and present personal and social relations, subjective experience as well as outer events and the agency of other people. Material adversity is important in interaction with personal circumstances. If poverty was the only cause of depression then all poor people would be depressed. This and later evidence demonstrate the role of social factors in psychopathology.

The advantage of the social causation model is that it exposes the role of material adversity, lack of direct economic power and social class effects. For example, not having access to the labour market is a vulnerability factor. Although child rearing is stressful for all parents, other contextual factors need to be taken into account to assess its impact on mental health. As working-class women also have a higher rate of severe events and major difficulties, they have a greater chance of experiencing both a provoking agent and a vulnerability factor. Brown and Harris's study indicates that at least in statistical terms, these considerations explain class difference in risk of depression among women with children.

The original model has been modified in the light of further data and conceptual influences from other sources. Brown et al. (1995) compared clinical and non-clinical populations in Islington, North London. Drawing on the work of Gilbert (1992) and Unger (1984) the authors elaborate their views concerning depression and the experience of life events. They conclude that the probability of depression increases not necessarily with loss or threatened loss *per se* but with the coexistence of humiliation and/or entrapment. The latter was also the final condition put forward by Bateson et al. (1956) when discussing the double bind in 'schizophrenia'. Thus, the ability of escape might be a protective factor in people who are at risk of depression or even a recovery factor in those already distressed.

The Islington study also highlights more details about the risk factors associated with adverse childhood experiences. A third of the depressed women had experienced neglect or abuse (physical or sexual) in childhood. This doubled the chances of these women becoming depressed as adults in any specific year, compared to those without such adverse antecedents (Bifulco et al. 1992). These childhood events also increase the probability of anxiety problems and could account for the common coexistence of depression and anxiety in adult patients (Brown 1996).

There have been some criticisms made about this study. First, the study is formulated within the positivist tradition: that is, the broad notion of 'psychiatric disorder' and the specific diagnosis of depression are discussed as if they have a universal and unproblematic status. Although Brown and Harris were aware of these difficulties they chose to retain the advantages of 'reducing the variety of psychiatric phenomena to a provisional order' (Brown and Harris 1978: 19). A second related criticism is the acceptance by Brown et al. 1995 of the psychiatric model. For example, they point out that social factors uncovered in the aetiology of depression need to be viewed as augmenting a biological disposition (Brown et al. 1995: 20). In the case of psychiatry itself, the professional interest served by the acceptance of versions of biological reductionism is clear. It is less clear why Brown, who is a sociologist, holds such a view. A third unintended problem that emerged after the Camberwell study was that its focus on women led to the danger of characterizing depression as a female condition. Although depression is diagnosed about twice as much in women than men (Comer 1998) and is the main reason why women are over-represented in psychiatric statistics, a research focus on women and depression may just add to a diagnostic bias.

Reviewing research studies that indicate an over-representation of women in mental health statistics, Busfield (1982) points out methodological problems with many of the research studies. The general problem of psychiatric epidemiology means that the over-representation of women could be a measurement artefact. For example in a study by Gove (1984) it was concluded that married women suffer higher levels of psychiatric morbidity than married men due to the added stress of the nurturing role of wife. When a wider range of diagnoses is considered, some studies indicate that the gap in representation between the genders almost disappears (Dohrenwend and Dohrenwend 1977; Regier et al. 1988). For example, men are more prone to acting out their distress in an anti-social way and have a higher incidence of drug and alcohol abuse. Consequently they are also more likely to receive a diagnosis of personality disorder whereas women are more likely to be self-harming and receive a diagnosis of depression.

Women are pathologized more readily than men. Society's view of normality is congruent with the stereotype of ideal masculinity (for example, assertive, independent, rational) whereas the ideal model of femininity held by society is defined as the opposite of the male ideal and includes attributes (for example, submissive, dependent) associated with vulnerability to distress (Broverman et al. 1970; Ussher 1991). Women are also more likely to disclose problems to professionals, and thus more likely to be labelled and recorded as patients. However, some argue that such findings reflect underlying sex-related assumptions held by clinicians making the diagnoses. Chessler (1972) and Ussher (1991) argue that male-dominated psychiatry pathologizes women's experiences in order to control their behaviour in line with stereotypes of femininity.

There has now been much research on the effects of physical and sexual abuse on women. In their review, Williams et al. (1993) conclude that at least 50 per cent of women who use community and hospital-based mental health services have been sexually or physically abused as children and as adults (Carmen et al. 1984; Beck and Van 1987; Bryer et al. 1987). There is also evidence that sexual and physical abuse is central to much that is diagnosed as severe mental illness (Herman et al. 1989), and that abuse is strongly linked with high service use (Walker and James 1992).

Some of these findings about women and mental health are supported from a different perspective, psychological rather than sociological, by many feminist writers within the psychoanalytical model (Mitchell 1975; Bordo 1979; Eichenbaum and Orbach 1982; Showalter 1987).

In a review of this literature, Busfield (1966) points out the strengths of this work. These include sensitivity to the complexities of inner life; elaboration of ways of understanding gender differences in symptomatology and its incorporation of the strengths of psychoanalysis such as in emphasizing the importance of childhood. However, Busfield also points to two major criticisms of feminist work written from within the perspective of the psychoanalytical model. The psychoanalytical model has left a legacy that leads to a limited conception of female experience and these limitations are reflected in many feminist studies influenced by the logic and concerns of psychoanalysis. There is a tendency to generalize about the human condition, and this weakness is not made less by focusing on women rather than the whole of humanity. It has produced a body of work insensitive to cultural diversity and the variability of experience created by race and class. A second criticism of feminist writers is that they follow the psychoanalytical model in ignoring the effect of external events in the real world on psychopathology. The psychological reductionism of the psychoanalysis is reflected in feminist writings.

Writers such as Busfield highlight how some research based on traditional objectivist/empirical methodology has offered a more sensitive, multi-layered and multi-faceted understanding of female experience in its social context than has the substantial work from the feminist perspective. For example the work of Brown and his colleagues can be situated within a Durkheimian positivist framework. Whatever the objectivist disadvantages of this tradition the work of Brown and Harris (1978) and Brown et al. (1995) brings alive both the mental life of women, and the current and past social situations that either protect or make them vulnerable to distress. By contrast, the subjectivism of feminist writers diverts attention from the external material factors that influence women's lives.

Race and ethnicity

The terms 'race' and 'ethnicity' are problematic notions that have been subjected to a number of definitions (see reviews by Omi and

Winant 1987; Hall 1988, 1989; Anthias 1992). The term 'race' is used to describe differences between people according to their external biological features, including and especially their skin colour. Given that outward manifestations of homo sapiens are not strictly or neatly divided but form a continuum, and people inter-marry between groups, there are good grounds for not making biological distinctions between people from all over the world. However, because race has also become a focus of identity (as with 'gender' it is a social and not a biological phenomenon) it remains a meaningful term retaining both a sociological and psychological salience. The term 'ethnicity' at its most general level refers to an identity that emerges from member-ship of a particular cultural and linguistic group or nationality. Ethnic positioning provides individuals with a way of interpreting the world, based on shared cultural resources and shared positioning relative to other groups. Thus, for example, while the Scots and French are predominantly both white skinned they belong to different ethnic groups. While considerable data has been accumulated on the 'visible minorities' in Britain, there has been a relative lack on the Celtic people of Britain. The few examples include Kenny (1985) on Irish and Davies (1999) on Welsh mental health.

Psychiatric and psychological research data has been accumulated about the Afro-Caribbean and Asian population. Studies of psychiatric epidemiology point to a mixed picture about the representation of Asian people. They also suggest that Asian patients admitted to hospital are more likely to be diagnosed as psychotic and treated with ECT than are white patients (Shaikh 1985). Some indicate over-representation for Pakistani immigrants (e.g. Carpenter and Brockin-ton 1980); others point to an under representation for Indian immigrants (Hitch 1981). Most of the research has focused on women (Krause 1989; Fenton and Sadiq 1993). Studies specifically focusing on the Afro-Caribbean population in Britain point to four main findings:

1. Although only around 5 per cent of the population is black, 25 per cent of patients on psychiatric wards with a diagnosis of schizo-phrenia are black (Banyard 1996). There is consistent evidence that Afro-Caribbean people are over-represented in admissions to psychiatric beds (Carpenter and Brockinton 1980; Dean et al. 1981). Whereas in Britain, 8 per cent of all psychiatric patients are detained compulsorily, up to 30 per cent of Afro-Caribbean patients are held against their will in in-patient settings at any point in time.

2. Young black men are referred to secure psychiatric settings via the courts 29 times more frequently than their white counterparts (Cope 1989) and are more likely to be subject to court orders requiring compulsory psychiatric treatment than whites (Browne 1990). They are more likely than whites to be apprehended by the police in public settings and referred by them for psychiatric assessment (Bean et al. 1991).
3. Afro-Caribbeans are more likely to be diagnosed as schizophrenic or other forms of psychotic illness (McGovern and Cope 1991) and are less likely to be diagnosed as depressed than white Britons (Chen et al. 1991).
4. They are more likely to receive physical treatment and less likely to receive psychological treatments than whites, with major tranquillizers and ECT being used with greater frequency (Littlewood and Cross 1980; Chen et al. 1991).

Several explanations for such findings have been proposed. Some advocates of the psychiatric model argue that there are real differences between ethnic groups citing, for example, the higher incidence of schizophrenia in black people. Once this argument is made then the other findings such as greater use of coercion and the use of major tranquillizers fall into place (Cope 1989). This type of explanation is in line with eugenic formulations which may be taken to suggest that black people are genetically vulnerable to severe mental illness. Another explanation centres on methodology rather than group differences as such, suggesting that psychiatrists, who are mostly white and middle class, misunderstand what is considered normal within the Afro-Caribbean culture as normal. For example, if symptoms of distress are not culturally understood this may lead to misdiagnosis of schizophrenia. A third group of explanations view the higher incidence of mental illness in ethnic minorities are a response to racism and disadvantage in a white dominated culture (Littlewood and Lipsedge 1982; Fernando 1988).

The arguments revolving around mental health problems in ethnic minorities raise some fundamental problems about psychiatric knowledge. As we describe in the next chapter, in Western discourse there is a tendency to assume that Western descriptions of the world are valid and superior to the constructions offered in other parts of the world. For example the notion of 'depression' is seen as valid and non-problematic. It is further assumed that it is universally encountered and experienced. Any deviation in expression from the Western norm is then described as a distortion of reality. Thus when

Asian people talk in terms, such as for example, 'a falling heart' this is construed by Western psychiatric commentators as a disguised or distorted (somatized) version of a 'true' condition – that is 'depression'. Krause (1989) and Fenton and Sadiq (1993) emphasize the centrality of the heart in South Asian culture so that there is a correspondence between 'the sinking heart' and sadness. Experientially one does not stand for the other; they are part of the same subjective state. The separation of bodily and mental distress is itself a product of Western Cartesian dualism although this separation is accorded the status of a universal 'fact'.

Although many studies purport to show diagnostic differences between racial groups, caution has to be exercised when considering mental health issues in different groups. Waters (1996) describes how many social psychiatric studies have made rash deductions and highlights the unsustainable attributions and generalizations which include the search for consistent patterns applicable to all in a specific ethnic group.

Further, as Fernando (1988) points out, the Western diagnostic research criteria used by conventional psychiatric research, fails to consider the cultural differences of the ethnic groups being studied. Factors such as cultural, social and economic influences need consideration for research into the mental health of ethnic minorities to have any validity. Smaje (1996) points out that adequate research on race, ethnicity and health should include factors such as genetics, migration, material factors, cultural factors and considerations of racism and discrimination.

Social constructivism and labelling theory

One of the most important theoretical perspectives in the sociological model of mental health and illness is social constructivism. The central assumption is that reality is not self-evident, stable and waiting to be discovered through some means of human endeavour.

Social constructionists who do not completely reject objectivist assertions concerning an objective reality, still view inherent difficulties in its conceptualization and definition. They view reality as being a product of human activity, that is, we socially construct a definition of reality. They also observe that power relationships are bound up with reality definitions such as the power to define, the power to influence, or the power to advance some interests at the expense of others.

This group of theorists questions the status of mental illness as a fact (Szasz 1961b). They analyse the ways in which mental health work has been linked to the production of psychiatric knowledge and the production of mental health problems (Parker et al. 1995). They also establish the links which exist in modern society between the coercive control of social deviance by psychiatry on the one hand and the professional role of mental health expertise on the other (Miller and Rose 1988).

The social constructivist approach does not necessarily have to be viewed as opposing social realism (the view that there is an independent existing reality) or the social causation approach (the view that social forces cause measurable phenomena to really exist). Although some social constructivists challenge both of these approaches (Gergen 1985) a number of writers who accept some constructivist arguments point out that strictly it is not reality that is socially constructed, but rather *theories* of reality (Greenwood 1994; Brown 1995).

This approach developed from the work of labelling theorists, and some view labelling theory as part of social constructivism. Labelling theory developed in the 1960s and has informed many other theories concerned with psychopathology. Many of its views have been assimilated into other models of psychopathology, in particular the socio-cultural. Labelling theory was concerned with documenting the ways in which the patient role was defined and maintained. The focus of study was on how others perceived, reacted to and categorized deviance. The wider theoretical context of this is the version of sociology called the 'symbolic interaction school', which is concerned with delineating the ways in which social reality is negotiated by people. Labelling theorists focus on the roles people take up and the meanings that are exchanged with others when occupying these roles. A failure to act appropriately in a role becomes a critical point of understanding for those involved.

Labelling theorists have outlined two forms of deviance, primary deviance and secondary deviance. When people deviate from conduct expected of them a common reaction of others is to deny the deviation by ignoring or rationalizing the behaviour, in order to keep the person in their existing role. For example, studies have been conducted that show that wives of men eventually labelled as schizophrenic and wives of husbands with drink problems ignored and rationalized their husbands' behaviour for various periods of time before seeking help (Yarrow et al. 1955). This is referred to as primary deviance, or variations in conduct that involve rule breaking.

Labelling theory is also concerned with how symptoms become diagnosed as mental illnesses so that the person takes on a deviant role, that is, secondary deviance. Scheff (1966) points out that mental disorder is 'residual deviance', or that which is left over after criminality and other bad conduct are considered but not attributed by observers. 'Schizophrenia' for Scheff is then the 'residue of the residues', a catch-all ascription of madness, when other forms of mental disorder had been considered and rejected.

Studies show that while behaviour under some circumstances will be ignored in other circumstances, the same behaviour can also provoke concern and the need for expert help. A study by Rosenhan (1973) highlighted the difficulties of diagnosis, as well as the difficulties in distinguishing normal from abnormal behaviour. In this study, a team of eight researchers visited twelve different mental hospitals, claiming as part of the study that they were experiencing auditory hallucinations and hearing voices saying words like 'dull' and 'thud'. They were not really hearing voices and answered all other questions asked by the medical staff honestly. However, most of the research team were admitted to hospital and diagnosed as schizophrenic. Once admitted, the task of the researchers was to convince the staff that they were sane, and while inside the hospital they behaved normally, insisting on their sanity. They were hospitalized for between 7 and 52 days with an average length of stay of 19 days. When discharged the researchers were diagnosed as schizophrenic in remission. While they were in hospital, their normal behaviours were perceived and interpreted by staff as being evidence of schizophrenia, although some of the other patients were able to identify the researchers as impostors. In the second part of the study, Rosenhan (1973, 1975) informed psychiatric hospitals that pseudo-patients would again present themselves at the hospitals over the next few months. In this part of the study there were no pseudo-patients, however, one fifth of patients admitted during this period were identified as pseudo-patients by staff. Rosenhan's studies are often taken as evidence of the uncertainty of diagnosis, how it can lead to labelling, and how once a label is attached to a person it becomes self-fulfilling. According to the societal reaction or labelling view the psychiatric patient's role is maintained by a new set of role expectations. The person designated as the patient plays the role of being a patient, while those looking on construe all of the person's conduct in terms of the patient role.

There have been several criticisms of labelling theory. Some point out that labelling theory understates the underlying power of the causes of primary deviation (Gove 1975). A second criticism is that the theory does not give a clear picture of what the salient contingencies are that make the difference between being ignored or being ascribed a label. However, there are some contingencies or circumstances that more regularly predict that the label of mental illness will be ascribed. For example, Horowitz (1983) points out that the greater the personal gap in terms of class, race, culture and gender between labellers and the potentially labelled, the greater the chances of ascription taking place and the more devaluing the label.

Schizophrenia

One of the most controversial issues in mental health is the nature of schizophrenia (Bentall 1990; Boyle 1991). It is the most common diagnosis given to those judged to be suffering from a 'major mental illness'. It is also the one that is given most commonly in young adulthood. Traditional psychiatric descriptions depict the schizophrenic as socially withdrawn suffering disturbances of cognitions (thought disorder or delusions), perceptions (hallucinations) and emotions ('flat' or 'inappropriate' affect).

Psychiatrists are divided or uncertain about the cause or nature of schizophrenia. Some view it as being genetically programmed, disturbing the brain and the person. Others follow the view of Winnicott (1958) that it is an environmental disease, resulting from poor maternal care in the first year of life, leaving the person psychologically vulnerable and without a secure sense of self. Others have attempted to render schizophrenic behaviour intelligible within the confused and confusing communication pattern of the patient's family (Laing and Esterson 1964). Due to weak aetiological agreement, schizophrenia is particularly vulnerable to labelling. Social constructivists criticize the conceptualization of schizophrenia (Bentall et al. 1988; Boyle 1991). Boyle notes that the conceptual weaknesses of the diagnosis is that it rests solely on symptoms. This means that it can only be validated tautologically. A person is said to be schizophrenic because of their oddity and they are deemed to be odd because they are suffering from schizophrenia.

The diagnosis of schizophrenia rests on value judgements about the person's unintelligible behaviour but does not have the equivalent of a blood test, as in the case, for example, of diabetes. Sociologists such as Coulter (1973) question how schizophrenia is ascribed. He argues that focusing on debates concerning aetiology obscures the ways in which madness emerges, first through social negotiation in the lay area and then in professional confirmation (a diagnosis). He describes the everyday expectations of normality and competence. With regard to hallucinations he points out that to maintain our credibility in a social group there has to be a consensus about what our senses detect around us. In most contexts, if a person sees or hears something which others do not, then their credibility and therefore their social group membership is jeopardized. However, it is possible in certain contexts that such idiosyncratic capacities might strengthen rather than weaken their credibility and group status. For example, Christian mystics and some African medicine men are expected to have visions. Indeed, their social credibility may rest on having these abnormal experiences. Al-Issa (1977) notes that, in Western society, hallucinations offend rationality. Surveys carried out on the general population estimate that between 10 per cent and 50 per cent of the 'normal' population hallucinate (Bentall and Slade 1985). Thus, atypical idiosyncratic perceptions are not intrinsically pathological although most Western psychiatrists claim that this is the case. Similarly, odd speech patterns are highly valued in some Christian sects that value the ability to 'speak in tongues' (Szasz 1992; Bentall and Pilgrim 1993). Such speech patterns may be reframed as evidence of schizophrenic thought disorder by a psychiatrist.

In Coulter's view there are no abstract defining qualities of schizophrenic thought but there are social settings in which the thoughts of some people are judged to be meaningless or illegitimate. From a sociological perspective knowledge of the norms of the society and the competencies of the individual are essential elements for a sociological consideration of concepts concerning psychopathology. While most cultures across time have some notion of oddity or madness, norms of sanity are not constant. Nor is there a trans-cultural or trans-historical consensus on what causes oddity or how to respond to it (Sedgwick 1982; Horowitz 1983). This undermines the claims of modern Western psychiatry that psychopathology and its symptoms are a stable set of factors that may be studied outside its wider context. It may also call into question the other models of psychopathology and their associated talking therapies that we have outlined.

The sociological perspectives described in this chapter are not limited to the field of sociological knowledge, but have been assimilated into other models of psychopathology, notably the socio-cultural model. It is these social-cultural critiques that we consider in the next chapter.

The socio-cultural model

The socio-cultural model is linked to the sociological model emphasizing how psychological problems are manifestations of disturbances in the social structures rather than of processes internal to the individual. Other perspectives, whether the lay view, legal framework or the psychiatric, psychoanalytical and psychological (cognitive-behavioural or humanistic) models of psychopathology, generally restrict their frame of reference to the individual or her/his immediate context. Socio-cultural explanations are less concerned with what constitutes psychiatric disorder and how the individual should be treated. Rather the model emphasizes the ways in which we are products of our culture, and as society precipitates psychopathology in the first place then society is the unit that needs treatment or change not the individual (for example, Newnes 1966). This model addresses issues such as how mental health professions themselves are part of the social forces operating on people, and whether the nature of therapy itself needs to change.

The social nature of the self

Socio-cultural analysis has been carried out on two levels. The first, on a micro level, considers the social nature of the self. The second concerns the effect of the wider social context on individual experience.

In a fundamental way it can be said that there is no such thing as the individual. In discussing the relationship between the individual and the social context, theorists from different disciplines, from different parts of the world and across time, arrive at the same general conclusions. The individual and the social context are inextricably woven together. Our sense of self is socially determined.

The social aspects of development are not completely ignored by the psychoanalytical school, as may be seen in Freud's emphasis on how the unique attributes of each person's ego and superego structures are determined to a great extent by the sorts of objects, such as parental models, that s/he had 'introjected', and how many parental values and prohibitions which were incorporated became forces that guided behaviour. Various terms used in psychoanalytical literature – such as internalization, introjection, identification, projection, transference – imply that the self involves the 'taking in' of attitudes, feelings, values and other aspects that initially derive from the other.

Generally, however, psychological approaches have confined themselves to considering the influences on human development of immediate relationships, such as with 'significant others' or the immediate family. This has led to serious limitations on the explanatory power of the theories it has produced. Some of the critical theorists derived from psychoanalysis have paid more attention to societal influences, for example Adler (1925), Horney (1939), Fromm (1941) and H.S. Sullivan (1953). These consider the influences that the wider society has on individual development and experience. However, for a more detailed analysis of how the individual and society are inextricably bound, we have to consider the models of social philosophy and psycholinguistics.

Psycholinguists such as Bakhtin (1981), Voloshinov (1976), Medvedev (in Bakhtin and Medvedev 1985) and Vygotsky (1939) all point to the social construction of experience. These writers made their contributions in the Soviet Union in the 1930s, and were undoubtedly influenced by the political and philosophical climate. One of Bakhtin's (1895–1975) basic tenets was that communicative acts only have meaning in particular social situations or contexts. Nothing demonstrates this principle more clearly than the fate of Bakhtin's own words, many of which were not heard in his own lifetime because they could not be published in the Soviet Union between 1929 and the 1960s. Soviet writers of that period stress the social context of experience and view language as an entirely social phenomenon. Vygotsky (1896–1934), in his book *Thought and Language* (1962), is concerned with the activity at the boundaries between people and their environment – with the psychological activities involved in making what is 'Other', or 'External' and

'Internal'. He emphasized that the organizing principles of thought and feeling rest in the structure of the shared language through which we express those thoughts and feelings.

Voloshinov viewed Freud as a representative of a wider intellectual trend that sought to explain and ground human behaviour in fundamentally biological, rather than social and historical terms. He replaced the Freudian concept of the unconscious with the multiplicity and contradictions of internalized social language. Working, in effect, from Freud's starting point of the patient's language and the talking cure, Voloshinov conceptualized the contents of the psyche as being made up of inner speech. Since language is inescapably social and occurs between people, the valuations of the social milieu reach to the core of the psyche. The conflicts and tensions of psychic life are not disputed, but they are recast as versions of the conflicts of the social milieu. In a similar way Smail, writing from a socio-cultural perspective, views a person's 'state of mind' as explainable through an understanding of the influences operating in the environmental space in which he or she is located.

Psycholinguists conceptualize the nature of the relationship between the individual and the social context as being so closely bound that to refer to an 'individual' in an absolute sense is a conceptual mistake or an error of categorization. These views may be summarized as follows:

1. The boundaries between what is outside and inside us are blurred. Language is at first outside the child who, through processes of physical maturation and social interaction, acquires language that becomes 'inside', part of the self;
2. Language forms part of the self or identity. It is how we speak to ourselves, form thoughts and concepts, and label thoughts and feelings. How our thoughts and feelings are organized, how we interpret events and ultimately what we do and do not perceive, all rest in the shared language through which we express them;
3. Words are formed in a social context and are carriers of social meaning. Experiences have meaning only when they are given a verbal label. It can only be through interaction with others that such labels and therefore meanings can be formed in the first place;
4. Words bear different inflections and emphases, and therefore different meanings, in different contexts;
5. The values of society are passed on to the individual through language. The values of the social context surrounding a language including cultural and historical factors, beliefs, attitudes and

ways of interpreting the world are passed down through language, making what is 'other' or 'external' to the individual 'internal'.

Our individuality or sense of self is essentially social in origin. In the most fundamental way what we perceive and believe, and how we view ourselves and our world, is based on social and cultural factors. Meaning, therefore, is socially negotiated.

Meaning systems

Edmund Husserl (1859–1938), a German mathematician and philosopher, may be described as the founder of phenomenology, the way we confer meaning upon the world. He inspired many philosophers, including Heidegger, Kierkegaard, Mead, Poole, Sartre and Merleau-Ponty and was the precursor of later psychological theories such as those of Allport, G.H. Kelly and Chomsky. A recurring theme in these theories is that meaning is socially negotiated, and conduct derives from the meanings that the person holds about the world. The social philosopher George Herbert Mead (1934) described how, in the full development of the self, the self is constituted by an organization of the particular attitudes of others towards him or her, and towards one another. His work was elaborated as part of the Chicago School of symbolic interactionism in the 1930s. Schwartz and Jacobs (1979) highlight three main principles from this approach. First, human conduct is a function of the meanings that the actor holds of the world. Second, these meanings arise from social interactions. Third, these meanings are maintained and modified through a process of interpretation within personal encounters.

Various terms have been used to describe an individual's meaning structure. The psychologist George Kelly (1955) described a person's 'personal construct system'. The sociologist Schutz (1962), applying the work of the philosopher Husserl, describes a person's 'repertoire of meanings', that are socially situated in time and place, so that at a given moment in time a culture will contain particular constructs or 'typifications' or a 'stock of knowledge' (Berger and Luckmann 1966).

These concepts of the social nature of the self and the negotiated communality of meaning systems are core concepts in the socio-cultural model of psychopathology, seen, for example, in the work of David Smail. He outlines how thought, memory, beliefs, perceptions, feelings or a person's 'state of mind' do not exist independently of the environment of which they are partly constituted. He emphasizes how any concept such as 'self' or 'personality' is socially determined and points out that as social beings we live according to shared rules of meaning. Nearly all the rules and concepts that shape and give meaning to our experience are not our personal inventions, but are acquired in the process of social development. Smail calls these rules and concepts, 'forms'. Our personal assimilation to, and adaptation of, these meaning systems is what is meant by our 'psychology'. Part of what an individual consists of is in fact non-individual, such as the social conventions practices, meanings and institutions we all share. Smail considers it a major error in most models of psychopathology to consider individual meaning-systems as belonging to and in the control of people of whom they form a part. Individuals cannot generally be expected to exercise a great deal of control over phenomena such as gender, socio-economic resources or ethnicity. For example, one's view of oneself as male or female is important to emotional well-being. This view is inseparable from the forms of masculinity and femininity that are culturally established independently of the individual. How far people are considered feminine or masculine depends on a form of femininity or masculinity that is outside them.

Political movements such as feminism are less likely to make the error of individualization because they do not take as a basic premise that each individual woman needs to change. Rather, feminism recognizes that for women to gain a more equitable share of social power requires a change in the forms relating to masculinity and femininity in our culture. Problems often arise when we cannot fulfil the demands of cultural forms.

In summary, language is one of the sets of rules that gives a form and meaning to our experience and is an intrinsic part of our sense of self. Meaning occurs within a social context that gives it a verbal construction and therefore a social reality. Cultural and historical factors, including beliefs and attitudes, are embedded in language and transmitted over time through the generations. Social and cultural values and norms are transmitted linguistically. If understanding one another is about exploring meaning systems, there is a need to represent or symbolize a person's experience, not to ignore it.

Cultural relativity and cultural autism

Just because a phenomenon is not verbally named by a society does not mean that it does not exist. Cultural autism or social muteness is reflected in individual understanding, so that the individual may also be rendered mute. For example, the phenomenon of childhood sexual abuse has always existed. However, it is only in the last decade or so that its prevalence has been generally articulated and acknowledged. Once acknowledged, the survivors of such abuse have come forward in significant numbers to request psychotherapy, and abuse is now given prominence as a major cause of distress. The same applies to many phenomena, such as that labelled shell shock in the First World War or more recent labelling of distress such as post-traumatic stress. Conversely, because a phenomenon is given a verbal label does not mean that it exists. The cultural relativity influencing our conceptions of psychopathology is emphasized by writers such as Szasz (1972) and Marshall (1966) who explore many of the myths behind our understandings of such constructs as psychosis, schizophrenia and mental illness.

Cultural factors influence how and what we see. As Husserl points out, the basic truth of perceptual experience is that what we see is directly dependent upon the perspective from which we see it. Although we are all conscious that there is only one world, we also see it differently, interpret it differently, and attribute different meanings to it at various times. In a process of selection and exclusion, a world-view will be filtered through the hopes and fears, the expectations and the experiences of the individual. The end result is a set of perspectives which have been multiply modified in the transmission. 'Meaning and interpretation belong together inseparably. Anything which visibly has a meaning is in that same instant invested with an interpretation by each and every onlooker' (Poole 1972: 6). The fact that we confer meaning on the world, instead of it imposing meaning on to us, implies that we are active participants in this process.

Following Husserl, Poole (1972) and Zukav (1979) point out there is no one single truth but only truths dependent upon the perspective from which we see it. What we term 'objectivity' consists of all the beliefs and unquestioned assumptions of a given society. Ignoring this essential fact is a serious error in the theories, clinical practice and research endeavours that describe models of psychopathology, an error reflected in conceptualizations of scientific paradigms and research methodologies. The current scientific paradigm individualizes science and ignores the fundamentally subjective and interactive nature of experience in its quest for so-called 'objectivity'.

This view, as we have seen in Chapter 7, is emphasized in labelling theory, concerned with societal reactions. Attempting to reduce everything to one reality or unreflectively asserting the importance of one reality over others has many critical implications. It affects the language we use, and ultimately all our thoughts and perceptions. Cultural factors are therefore embedded in and shape what we think we 'know'. In turn this gives legitimacy to certain forms and content of 'knowledge'. Sayal (1989), writing on black women and mental health, illustrates some of the issues: there are often sweeping generalizations made about black people, that, for example, 'passive' Asian women are subjected to oppressive practices within the family, or that Afro-Caribbean women are strong and dominant.

Stereotypes are accepted as 'facts' and are frequently used by mental health workers. Sayal claims that by accepting pathologizing notions about 'black families' we collude with the pseudo-science that gives legitimacy to popular racism, since we make presumptions about homogeneity that we do not make about white families. This process is seen at the level of professional 'science', for example, in concepts such as 'ethnicity' and 'transcultural psychiatry'. An examination of the studies conducted in this area suggests that most of the studies claiming to be on black family life are actually concerned with poverty. Sayal points out that the poor are frequently identified as ' "culturally deprived" . . . so that poverty is discussed as if it is a personal trait rather than a social condition, and deviations from ethnocentric norms are viewed as deprivation' (1989: 4). A consequence of this is that a high proportion of black children are in care because black women are viewed as unfit for mothering, and until recently as unfit for fostering and adoption. Sayal also describes how psychiatric formulations are made of black-specific mental illnesses, such as 'West Indian psychosis'. The psychiatric theories which claimed that black genes were causal factors in mental illness have now been substituted by theories which view black culture as a causal factor in mental illness.

Many of the values we hold in Western society about the goals of psychotherapy are themselves potentially culturally specific. Therapy focuses on the individual with for example, restoring 'a sense of autonomy' or 'taking responsibility for the self', set as goals of treatment. Other cultures take a different approach to therapy. A Hindu in India might instead be helped to reintegrate within their social group and to restore the sense of interdependence rather than independence.

Our cultural context therefore shapes how we think about psychopathology. What are taken to be 'facts' in mental health are culturally determined. Definitions and classifications are not absolute but change across cultures across time. Albee (1996) gives the example of the psychiatric view of homosexuality. The first edition of DSM classified homosexuality as a sexual deviation. However, in 1973 the second edition of DSM was modified when the American Psychiatric Association eliminated the general category of homosexuality as a mental disorder, unless it was distressing to the person concerned. Thus, in the 1970s, thousands of US citizens were changed overnight from being defined as mentally ill to normal.

Psychological distress or symptoms of psychopathology are manifested differently in different socio-cultural contexts. A syndrome traditionally not seen in Western cultures is 'amok', where men erupt, following a period of depression and brooding, into a sudden state of frenzied and unprovoked indiscriminate violence ending in exhaustion and amnesia. The condition has traditionally been associated with the Malayan people and was relatively common a few hundred years ago, although rare today. Theorists have speculated that amok was related to the cultural values that placed heavy restrictions on adolescents and adults and the belief in magical possession by demons and evil spirits. There are other culture-bound syndromes (see Westermeyer 1985), and, even when similar psychological problems are seen in different parts of the world, the way a particular syndrome is perceived may vary from culture to culture (Erinosho and Ayonrinde 1981).

The individualization of distress

Even though in the different models of psychopathology there are a variety of theoretical ideas and practical procedures, many of them markedly incompatible with each other, there are nevertheless some general issues common to most models that distinguish them from the socio-cultural model.

A major criticism that may be made of models of psychopathology generally is that they are inherently too individualistic from their theoretical conceptualizations to their practical applications. The reductionist view of science prevalent within our culture is reflected in the empirical research paradigm of contemporary psychology and psychiatry. This research is used to legitimize the current models of psychopathology and confer validity on their theoretical underpinnings.

Chomsky (1968) and Poole (1972) point out that science is inadequate when it focuses on selected parts rather than the totality of problems. Poole defines an adequate science as 'the study of the totality of problems, objective and subjective, by the whole thinker, taking into account all the evidence, both quantifiable and unquantifiable' (Poole 1972: 108–9). However the traditional scientific paradigm of empirical research emphasizes an analysis and solution of problems, and ignores wider contextual issues. This type of research into human behaviour is seen, for example, in the geneticists' quest to isolate genes for happiness, aggression, and so on; as well as in psychiatric and psychological researchers isolating specific symptoms, or specific events of the therapeutic process, or isolating the client and/or therapist from the total subjective context within which therapy takes place. It is questionable whether these different frameworks actually help clients to understand the source of their unhappiness, or merely elevate the notion of illness. Writers such as Masson (1990, 1991), Heath (1992), Smail (1987, 1993) and Szasz (1971) point out the inappropriate therapies and treatments given for conditions of which we do not know the fundamental causes, but which may turn out to be psycho-social in origin. They draw attention to the inappropriate and inadequate view of the nature of the self that ignores political, economic and cultural sources of pain and distress and which avoids any real analysis and criticism of a social order based on inequality of wealth, opportunity and choice. They challenge the view that focuses, simplistically, on individuals and families as the target of intervention. In therapy, while close attention is paid to personal and interpersonal processes, the focus is on the significance of events in particular, isolated contexts. For example, Masson criticizes Freud for his inherently individualistic view in ignoring external sources of distress, stating: 'Freud is asking us to shift the direction of our attention, from the external to the internal. Freud was perpetuating a tradition that did not begin with him. Its basic characteristics were that it was male-oriented, ethnocentric, sexist, and rigidly hierarchical' (1991: 208).

Models of psychopathology view the cause of distress as being due to some deficit or fault located within the individual's psyche or biochemistry, or as an inadequacy in coping with external situations rather than the cause of distress being located in the wider context. The different models concentrate on the significance of events in particular isolated contexts; for example, bio-medical models concentrate on a specific symptom, or set of symptoms, while cognitive and behavioural models focus on specific behaviours and dysfunctional thought patterns. In the psychoanalytic model and its derivatives, close attention is given to the unconscious, to transference or shifts in group dynamics, and so on. When wider influences are considered, this is usually confined to issues close to the individual's immediate context such as a consideration of relationships within the family; or what is described about such circumstances is viewed and interpreted by therapists in symbolic or iconic forms, rather than as the literal or material reality experienced and described by the patient. This has led to serious limitations of the explanatory power of models of psychopathology theories and practical applications that have been derived from them.

The ethos of individualism is also reflected in the institutional and professional cultures of our working environment, and a sociopolitical system that emphasizes individual effort and responsibility. Smail (1993) documents how psychotherapy, psychology and psychiatry have helped shape a culture of individualism where it has become almost impossible for people to differentiate inside from outside, or to attribute the pain they often feel about themselves to its appropriate source. We often wrongly locate the origins or 'cause' of our pain as being located inside us and as being a reflection of our own inadequacy or personal failing.

Traditional and contemporary bio-medical and psychological models of psychopathology tend not to recognize that distress is often caused by a person finding that they are unable to meet the requirements of what Smail terms 'form'. For example, we cannot change homosexuality to heterosexuality. While mental health practitioners no longer expect their clients to be able to alter their sexual preferences at will they still often assume that people have access 'within' them to forms of behaviour which are more 'adjusted' than those they are currently displaying; and all that is needed is some kind of individualistic enterprise usually framed in terms such as 'moral effort', 'cognitive understanding or restructuring', 'emotional insight' or the 'medication of choice' or 'taking responsibility'.

It is often the absence of form in our rapidly changing mobile society that leads to distress. For example there are few forms to guide our relationships with each other in modern Western society. To acquire new forms when the old ones have disappeared or disintegrated may or may not be possible. When an individual's experience cannot receive its meaning from an appropriate public form – the result is often pain, including forms of pain such as blame and guilt. People find themselves isolated with feelings, impulses, ideas or thoughts that are not reflected in formal public concepts or meanings. Often they will then seek help from a psychiatric and therapeutic industry only too ready to produce a formal diagnosis for their difficulty.

One implication of this is that symptoms of pathology or variations in the expressions of human distress are not constant, but fluctuate according to what is happening in the social environment. Numerous community studies point out that the prevalence of psychological distress is as great as 18 to 20 per cent of the population. Given these figures, as the work of the American community psychologist George Albee (1996) emphasizes, it is both practically and ethically unreasonable to suggest that the distress of such a high proportion of the population should be viewed as evidence of psychopathology.

However, since neither the causes nor cures of distress are, in the socio-cultural model, just an individual matter, clinicians may only alleviate some of the painful consequences of distress. Writers such as Davies (1995), Richards (1995) and Pilgrim (1997) point out that the explanations have limited relevance where there is little or no understanding of the individual's cultural and social context. Others, such as Pillay (1993) suggest that greater knowledge of the social and economic reality would be more useful in understanding psychological processes, than assuming culturally based psychosis in Afro-Caribbeans and somatization in Asians. As Sayal, states: 'As a clinician, I think it is crucial to relate personal misery to its environment, history and political context. If you rob a person of their history, you rob them of their sense of self' (1989: 6).

Therapy as oppression

The socio-cultural model questions our perceptions of what is normal and abnormal and our use of power over others. By individualizing distress and locating the problem as somehow located within the person rather than in the wider social structure, mental health workers can be viewed as agents of social control. According to some critics, therapy of whatever theoretical model is an oppressive and abusive force that maintains the political status quo (Masson 1988). Heath comments on the way clinicians, 'do this by individualizing problems and by putting the emphasis on the individual to improve. Put succinctly: psychiatry and psychotherapy perpetuate social oppression by abuse of power' (1992: 3).

Ignoring the cultural context of someone's life involves the imposition of one particular reality on another. The therapeutic situation is one where power resides with the therapist, 'the expert' who can impose his or her view of reality on the client (Masson 1990). They may do this unintentionally by simply ignoring the cultural context of the patient's life. Heath accepts that this form of oppression is rarely intentional, or carried out of malevolent motives: 'I do not need to be malevolent in order to oppress people. I can oppress people with the best of intentions out of ignorance and I may perpetuate my ignorance to protect my power' (1992: 33).

Dorothy Rowe, in her foreword to Masson's book, states, 'In the final analysis, power is the right to have your definition of reality prevail over all other people's definition of reality' (Masson 1990: 16). The type of approach selected by or selected for individuals defines reality within one particular frame of reference. Clinicians present their version of reality as being akin to some kind of ultimate truth. However Karasau (1986) reports 400 different schools, with their corresponding views on the reality and human experience. As Rowe states: 'It is a good rule of thumb that if many treatments are in use for the same disease it is because there is no real treatment known for that disease' (1991: 370).

Such criticisms of psychotherapy might also be applied to clinical research. Research can serve self-interest at an implicit and explicit level. This is not generally intentional but merely reflects an unquestioning acceptance of the traditional scientific paradigm. For example, some critics (Rose 1990; Marshall 1996) draw attention to erroneous conclusion derived from the statistical techniques used in research methodology. Further, Marshall (1996) comments on the research process into the psychiatric diagnosis of 'schizophrenia' describing how first the label becomes seemingly scientifically validated as an 'illness' then reified into a mainly genetic disorder that then justifies the search for specific causal genes: 'much of what passes for science here is a myth-making process which develops a momentum of its own, powered by a variety of interests, and supported by a lack of real analysis and an inclination to provide results which support a biologically determinist stance' (Marshall 1996: 5). At a more explicit level, although science may aspire to principles of objectivity, there is no doubt that in practice scientific research may be influenced by wider political agendas of funding. For example, Breggin (1993) and Marshall (1996) discuss unintentional and intentional consequences of the relationship between clinical research and the psychopharmaceutical industry. Research generally is sometimes driven by self interest and other human failings rather than a search for truth, and therapy research is no different (Goldfried 2000) despite the huge amount of psychological research findings (Bergin and Garfield 1994).

Conclusion

The socio-cultural model emphasizes the limitations of psychiatric and psychological models as an answer to emotional distress, urges caution upon the different explanations for manifestations of distress. Smail questions whether psychology and psychiatry have any relevance at all to issues that are, essentially, political in nature but does not reject psychotherapy and counselling completely. Instead he emphasizes that we need to be mindful of their limitations as in some instances, the claims of psychotherapy have often seemed ambitious to the point of grandiosity.

All clinicians try to distance themselves from the risk that they may increase the incidence of the very social ills whose effects they are trying to alleviate. Through neglecting the wider social context in which the illnesses arise and have meaning, they perpetuate the state of illness-making contexts. An appropriate assessment of patients should at the very least consider the resources available to them (such as their economic situation, emotional and social supports), and the constraints that limit their lives (such as the lack of positive resources and institutional constraints). The effects of these constraints are seen in all aspects of life and in all relationships, from personal relationships, to relationships with societal structures such as school, family and public institutions.

Adherents of the socio-cultural model of psychopathology point out that consideration of the nature of the distress of clients would often highlight a fundamental economic cause. For many professionals this is a difficult issue to confront as it at times questions their professional and personal agenda and the efficacy of their models. It also conflicts with the institutional and professional cultures, the working environment and the present political, moral and intellectual climate. This way of conceptualizing and dealing with distress or psychopathology is further supported by mental health institutions that encourage a throughput of 'cured' patients, carefully evaluated and reasonably satisfied with the service they receive.

Socio-cultural theorists highlight how society has become more individualized and how more people view their particular suffering as a unique, individual problem for which they are told to seek professional help. However this further isolates sufferers in their distress. Meanwhile the traditional means of comfort, solace and communal sharing are lost as the solutions to distress are professionalized.

What therapists can do to change society is limited. However, there have been some attempts to address the wider social context of clients, and writers such as Heath (1992) and Smail (1987) point to ways forward in therapy. A more equitable therapeutic endeavour would include an awareness of the pervasive effects of cultural and social issues manifested in the debilitating effects on the individual's sense of self, in institutions and in interpersonal relationships, including some therapeutic relationships. There are also ways of offering more appropriate forms of help and promoting a better therapeutic outcome, although in many instances the most important positive developments have been outside the statutory services, in self-help groups, crisis lines and intervention services such as the White City Project (Holland 1992), the Newpin Project (Newpin 1992) and the Shanti Project (Mills 1992). Such examples of community psychology use mass media campaigns or educational programmes in schools to help prevent some of the problems from arising in the first place.

In this and the previous chapter we have described the serious questions that need to be asked about the attempt to identify psychopathology – at least to identify it within the individual, or within the network of their immediate relationships. The socio-cultural model has this in common with psychoanalysis, psychiatry, the less exploratory versions of clinical psychology and the humanistic therapies: that it takes just as much interest in what the patient is saying. Different models of psychopathology treat words as information to build up an expert formulation, even if some psychiatrists rely overmuch on symptoms. But clearly the way words are understood, and meaning is attached to them, affects the therapist as much as the patient. If a distinction can be made at all between the more prescriptive approaches in psychiatry and clinical psychology on the one hand, and exploratory psychotherapies on the other, it is that in the broader autobiographical interest of the latter the shifting meanings negotiated in the relationship are more complex and open-ended. The socio-cultural model attends to yet different signals, which are to do with the more pervasive stresses in society and its culture.

However, the socio-cultural model is also a construct, and it may serve the interests of its theorists as much as any other model of psychopathology. As von Bertalanffy observes:

> All scientific constructs are models representing certain aspects or perspectives of reality. This even applies to theoretical physics: far from being a metaphysical presentation of ultimate reality (as the materialism of the past proclaimed and modern positivism implies) it is but one of those models and, as recent developments show, neither exhaustive nor unique. (1987: 62)

CHAPTER 9

Conclusion

As we have described in this book there are many different ways of conceptualizing psychopathology reflecting differing notions of normality and abnormality, and differing perceptions of the nature and meaning of manifestations of psychological distress in society. Historically, psychopathology has been understood in many ways such as it being the result of supernatural forces or demonic possession. At various times manifestations of psychopathology have attracted ridicule, fear, pity and anger. At the most general level psychopathology is used as a term to refer to those thoughts, feelings, and behaviours that are unusual or distressing to the individual, are perhaps dangerous to the person or to others, or viewed as strange or unusual in some way by the society. Essentially these people are seen as different to most other people.

Each model we have described, defines the term psychopathology within its own frame of reference. We have pointed out some of the difficulties in drawing a clear distinction between what might be considered as normal and abnormal behaviour. Considerations of what is regarded as normal and what is abnormal are not value free, a particular concern for those working within the sociological and socio-cultural models. Terms such as 'abnormality' carry strong negative connotations. Hence writers such as Comer (1998) suggest the use of different terminology, terms that indicate whether a person's thoughts, feelings or behaviour are distressing, dangerous, deviant or dysfunctional. The more extreme these are and the more obvious to others the more likely we are to consider them as manifestations of psychopathology. These are useful concepts when considering what constitutes an abnormal psychological condition, although it remains difficult to draw a clear boundary between abnormality and normality.

We have outlined the frames of reference and underlying concepts of the main models of psychopathology and their developments. These are the psychiatric and bio-medical models, variants of the psychoanalytic (including attachment theory), behavioural, cognitive, humanistic and sociological/socio-cultural models. Each model offers a version of reality and a set of assumptions underlying its understanding of human nature, differing perspectives concerning the nature of psychopathology and different explanations concerning the cause of psychological distress. Each model also offers a different understanding of the mechanisms which lead one person and not another to develop psychological problems.

The psychiatric/bio-medical model suggests that psychological problems are the result of biochemical imbalances in the brain or some physical dysfunction, the psychoanalytic model that psychological problems are caused by unconscious conflicts and repressed wishes as well as difficulties in infancy and childhood, while the behavioural model suggests that psychological problems are the result of maladaptive learning. The cognitive model views psychological problems as caused by irrational or distorted thinking, and the humanistic model by thwarted personal growth, reflecting a failure to know and accept oneself. The sociological and socio-cultural models suggest that psychological problems result from damaging social and economic factors.

As well as the causes of psychopathology the different models conceptualize solutions to alleviate the manifestations of psychopathology. Historically, the solutions to psychological distress have reflected views about psychopathology, including attempts to exorcise demons or taking cold baths. Contemporary models of psychopathology continue to influence the development of psychological therapies aiming to alleviate psychological problems. Many of these approaches stress active participation of the patient or client, although change in wider social structures is emphasized by the sociological critiques and the socio-cultural model, while the bio-medical model, still the major treatment offered by psychiatry, emphasizes chemical imbalance and the need for physical treatment. All of these models inform us about human experience and how psychopathology may develop, and the talking therapies cannot afford to neglect the bio-medical or social aspects. We are biological beings who live in a social world and the importance of both biology and society need to be considered when discussing the causes of and solutions to human distress.

One of the themes we have raised while discussing differing perspectives is the nature and status of scientific enquiry. While some models emphasize how the scientific method helps us verify what we think to be true, others question traditional views as to what constitutes an adequate science. In Chapter 2 we described how the bio-medical and medical approaches emphasize the scientific role of classification, and the use of experimental methods to test out different hypotheses including the effectiveness of particular treatments. In Chapter 3 we described Freud's initial emphasis on a scientific approach and outlined later criticisms concerning the scientific status of psychoanalytical approaches. In the chapter on behavioural and cognitive approaches we drew attention to the emphasis upon the traditional notions of science and hypothetic-deductive methodology. These models stress the necessity of defining observable and measurable behaviour in their conceptualizations of psychopathology. However, when considering some of the formulations in the humanistic model in Chapter 7 we showed how some of the ideas about human nature do not lend themselves easily to the application of traditional scientific methodology. Finally by examining the sociological and socio-cultural models it may be seen that despite the aim of the scientific method to be objective, what we know is often strongly influenced by the values of our society.

Traditional scientific method supposedly allows us to verify the validity of what we think is true. In many ways we see what we want to or expect to see. Carl Rogers (1961) stated: 'Scientific research needs to be seen for what it truly is; a way of preventing me from deceiving myself in regard to my creatively formed subjective hunches which have developed out of the relationship between me and my material.' Thus he advises adherence to the scientific paradigm so as not to deceive ourselves. However, as we have described in these chapters, there has been much discussion as to the nature of an adequate science and the limitations of traditional scientific methodology especially when applied to the study of human beings. Further, adherents of the socio-cultural model criticize many findings based on traditional scientific methodology pointing to the misuse of statistical techniques in some studies and implicit political agendas of others. Scientists, like everyone else, find it difficult to relinquish what they believe to be true.

The main frameworks or models in which psychopathology has been conceptualized has led to many elaborations, amendments and developments. Further, many contemporary views of psychopathology and therapy adopt and adapt concepts from different models, resulting in an interweaving of ideas. Many have questioned whether any one model is enough to explain all the different ways in which psychopathology is expressed. Mental health workers would possibly point out that human experience is so diverse that no one model is able to offer the full explanation of all psychological problems of all of the people all of the time. Thus some therapists work in an eclectic way – drawing on the techniques and interventions associated with one therapeutic approach when they see it as appropriate. Other therapists describe themselves as integrative, weaving together two or more models that have some consistency with each other. Surveys suggest that at least one third of therapists describe themselves as either eclectic or integrative (Prochaska and Norcross 1999).

The different models of psychopathology we have outlined do not represent exclusive categories. However, rather than assume that there are competing claims about the same issue, or set of issues, we need to reflect on different frameworks or models of understanding. Each of the models of psychopathology has strengths and weaknesses. What we may conclude is that these different models of psychopathology warn us against drawing firm conclusions, and remind us to go on questioning our own beliefs and assumptions.

References

Adler, A. (1925) *The Practice and Theory of Individual Psychology*. New York: Harper.

Adorno, T.W., Frenkel-Brunswick, E., Levinson, D.J. and Sanford, R.N. (1950) *The Authoritarian Personality*. New York: Harper and Brothers.

Ahlburg, D.A. and Shapiro, D.O. (1983) The darker side of unemployment, *Hospital and Community Psychiatry*, 34: 389.

Ainsworth, M.D.S. (1967) Infancy in Uganda: Infant care and the growth of attachment, in A. Ambrose (ed.) *Stimulation in Early Infancy*. London: Academic Press.

Ainsworth, M.D.S. (1969) Object relations, dependency, and attachment: A theoretical review of the infant-mother relationship, *Child Development*, 40: 969–1025.

Ainsworth, M.D.S. (1979) Infant–mother attachment, *American Psychologist*, 34: 932–7.

Ainsworth, M.D.S. (1985) Attachment across the lifespan, *Bulletin of the New York Academy of Medicine*, 61: 792–812.

Ainsworth, M.D.S. (1990) Some considerations regarding theory and assessment relevant to attachments beyond infancy, in M.T. Greenberg, D. Ciccetti and E.M. Cummings (eds) *Attachment in the preschool years*. Chicago: University of Chicago Press.

Ainsworth, M.D.S., Blehar, M.C., Waters, E. and Wall, S. (1978) *Patterns of attachment: A psychological study of the strange situation*. Hillsdale, NJ: Erlbaum.

Albee, G.W. (1996) Searching for the magic marker. Paper presented at the J. Richard Marshall Memorial Conference of the Psychotherapy Section of the British Psychological Society, Nottingham, 27 April.

Albee, G.W. (2000) The boulder model's fatal flaw, *American Psychologist*, 55: 247–8.

Al-Issa, I. (1977) Social and cultural aspects of hallucinations, *Psychological Bulletin*, 84: 570–87.

American Psychiatric Association (1994) Diagnostic and Statistical Manual of Mental Disorders, 4th edn. Washington, DC: American Psychiatric Association.

Ammaniti, M., van Ijszendoorn, M.H., Speranza, A.M. and Tambelli, R. (1998) *Internal Working Models of Attachment During Late Childhood and Early Adolescence: An Exploration of Stability and Change.* Manuscript submitted for publication.

Anderson, E.M. and Lambert, M.J. (1995) Short-term dynamically orientated psychotherapy: A review and meta-analysis, *Clinical Psychology Review,* 15: 503–14.

Anthias, F. (1992) Connecting race and ethnic phenomena, *Sociology,* 26(3): 421–38.

Argyle, M. (1994) *The Psychology of Social Class.* London: Routledge.

Arlow, J.A. and Brenner, C. (1969) The psychopathology of the psychoses: A proposed revision, *Int. J. Psychoanalysis,* 50: 5–14.

Ashton, H. (1991) Psychotropic drug prescribing for women, *British Journal of Psychiatry,* 158: 30–5.

Baker-Miller, J.B. (1971) Psychological consequences of sexual inequality, *American Journal of Orthopsychiatry,* 41: 767–75.

Bakhtin, M.M. (1981) *The Dialogic Imagination: Four Essays.* Texas: University of Texas Press.

Bakhtin, M.M. and Medvedev, P.N. (1985) *The Formal Method in Literary Scholarship: A Critical Introduction to Sociological Poetics.* Harvard: Harvard University Press.

Baldwin, M.W. (1992) Relational schemas and the processing of social information, *Psychological Bulletin,* 112: 461–84.

Balint, M. (1968) *The Basic Fault.* New York: Brunner/Mazel.

Bandura, A. (1969) *Principles of Behavior Modification.* New York: Holt, Rinehart and Winston.

Bandura, A. and Walters, R.H. (1963) *Social Learning and Personality Development.* New York: Ronald Press.

Bannister, D. (1960) Conceptual structure in thought disordered schizophrenics, *Journal of Mental Science,* 106: 1230–49.

Bannister, D. (1965) The rationale and clinical relevance of repertory grid technique, *British Journal of Psychiatry,* 11: 977–82.

Bannister, D. (1966) A new theory of personality, in B. Foss (ed.) *New Horizons in Psychology.* Harmondsworth: Penguin.

Bannister, D. (1968) The logical requirements of research into schizophrenia, *British Journal of Psychiatry,* 114: 1088–97.

Bannister, D. (1983) The internal politics of psychotherapy, in D. Pilgrim (ed.) *Psychology and Psychotherapy.* London: Routledge and Kegan Paul.

Bannister, D. and Fransella, F. (1965) A repertory grid test of schizophrenic thought disorder, *British Journal of Social and Clinical Psychology,* 2: 95–102.

Bannister, D. and Salmon, P. (1966) Schizophrenic thought disorder: Specific or diffuse? *British Journal of Medical Psychology,* 39: 215–19.

Banyard, P.E. (1996) *Applying Psychology to Health*. London: Hodder and Stoughton.

Barlow, D.H., Craske, M.G., Cerny, J.A. and Klosko, J.S. (1989) Behavior treatment of panic disorder, *Behavior Therapy*, 20: 261–82.

Baruch, G. and Treacher, A. (1978) *Psychiatry Observed*. London: Routledge and Kegan Paul.

Bassett, A.S., McGillivray, B.C., Jones, B.D. and Pantzar, J.T. (1988) Partial trisomy chromosome 5 cosegregating with schizophrenia, *Lancet*, 108: 799–801.

Bassuk, E., Rubin, L. and Lauriat, A. (1984). Is homelessness a mental health problem? *American Journal of Psychiatry*, 141: 1546–51.

Bateson, G., Jackson, D., Haley, J. and Weakland, J. (1956) Towards a theory of schizophrenia, *Behavioral Science*, 1: 251–64.

Bean, P. (1980) *Compulsory Admissions to Mental Hospital*. Chichester: Wiley.

Bean, P., Bingley, W., Bynoe, I., Rasseby, E. and Rogers, A. (1991) *Out of Harm's Way*. London: MIND.

Bebbington, P.E., Hurry, J. and Tennant, C. (1981) Psychiatric disorders in selected immigrant groups in Camberwell, *Social Psychiatry*, 16: 43–51.

Beck, A.T. and Emery, G. (1985) *Anxiety Disorders and Phobias: A Cognitive Perspective*. New York: Basic.

Beck, A.T. and Freeman, A. (1990) *Cognitive Therapy of Personality Disorders*. New York: Guilford.

Beck, J.C. and Van, D.K.B. (1987) Reports of childhood incest and current behavior of chronically hospitalised psychotic women, *American Journal of Psychiatry*, 144 (11): 1474–6.

Belsky, J. and Nezworski, T. (eds) (1988) *Clinical Implications of Attachment*. Hillsdale, NJ: Erlbaum.

Belsky, J., Rosenberg, K. and Cmic, K. (1995) The origin of attachment security: Classical and contextual determinants, in S. Goldberg, R. Muir and J. Kerr (eds) *Attachment Theory: Social, Developmental, and Clinical Perspectives*. Hillsdale, NJ: Analytic Press.

Bentall, R.P. (ed.) (1990) *Reconstructing Schizophrenia*. London: Routledge.

Bentall, R.P., Jackson, H. and Pilgrim, D. (1988) Abandoning the concept of schizophrenia: some implications of validity arguments for psychological research into psychotic phenomena, *British Journal of Clinical Psychology*, 27: 303–24.

Bentall, R.P. and Pilgrim, D. (1993) Thomas Szasz, crazy talk and the myth of mental illness, *British Journal of Medical Psychology*, 66: 69–76.

Bentall, R.P. and Slade, P. (1985) Reality testing and auditory hallucinations: a signal detection analysis, *British Journal of Clinical Psychology*, 24: 150–69.

Beres, D. (1956) Ego deviation and the concept of schizophrenia, *The Psychoanalytical Study of the Child*, (12).

Berger, P. and Luckman, B. (1966) *The Social Construction of Reality*. New York: Doubleday.

Bergin, A. and Garfield, S. (1994) (eds) *Handbook of Psychotherapy and Behavior Change*. New York: Wiley.

Berne, E. (1964) *Games People Play*. New York: Grove Press.

Berne, E. (1971) Away from a theory of the impact of interpersonal interaction on non-verbal participation, *Transactional Analysis Journal*, 1: 6–13.

Bifulco, A., Harris, T.O. and Brown, G.W. (1992) Mourning or inadequate care? Re-examining the relationship of maternal loss in childhood with adult depression and anxiety, *Development and Psychopathology*, 4: 433–49.

Bion, W.R. (1959) *Experiences in Groups*. New York: Basic Books.

Blaxter, M. (1990) *Health and Lifestyle*. London: Routledge.

Bleuler, E. (1911/1991) *Dementia Praecox, or the Group of Schizophrenias*. Madison, CT: International University Press.

Bordo, S. (1979) 'Material Girl': the effacements of post-modern culture, in C. Schwichitenberg (ed.) *The Madonna Connection*. Boulder, CO: Westview.

Bowlby, J. (1944) Forty-four juvenile thieves: Their characters and home life, *International Journal of Psycho-Analysis*, 25: 19–52, 107–27.

Bowlby, J. (1946) *Forty-four Juvenile Thieves: Their Characters and Home-life*. London: Baillière, Tindall and Cox.

Bowlby, J. (1956) The growth of independence in the young child, *Royal Society of Health Journal*, 76: 587–91.

Bowlby, J. (1958) The nature of the child's tie to his mother, *International Journal of Psycho-Analysis*, 39: 350–73.

Bowlby, J. (1960) Separation anxiety, *International Journal of Psycho-Analysis*, 41: 1–25.

Bowlby, J. (1969/1982) *Attachment and Loss: Vol. 1. Attachment*. New York: Basic Books.

Bowlby, J. (1973) *Attachment and Loss: Vol. 2. Separation*. New York: Basic Books.

Bowlby, J. (1980) *Attachment and Loss: Vol. 3. Loss*. New York: Basic Books.

Boyle, M. (1990) *Schizophrenia: A Scientific Delusion?* London: Routledge.

Bozarth, J.D. (1998) *Person-centred Therapy: A Revolutionary Paradigm*. Ross-on-Wye: PCCS Books.

Breen, R. and Rottman, D. (1955) Class analysis and class theory, *Sociology*, 29(3): 453–73.

Breggin, P. (1993) *Toxic Psychiatry*. London: Fontana.

Bretherton, I. (1985) Attachment theory: Retrospect and prospect, in I. Bretherton and E. Waters (eds) Growing points of attachment theory and research. *Monographs of the Society for Research in Child Development*, 50(1–2, Serial No. 209): 3–38.

Bretherton, I. (1990) Open communication and internal working models: Their role in the development of attachment relationships, in R.A. Thompson (ed.) *Nebraska Symposium on Motivation: Vol. 36. Socioemotional development*. Lincoln: University of Nebraska Press.

Bretherton, I. and Waters, E. (1985) Growing points in attachment theory and research. Monographs of the Society for Research in Child Development, 50 (1–2, Serial No. 209).

Brisman, J. (1992) Bulimia in the late adolescent: An analytic perspective to a behavior problem, in J. O'Brien, D. Pilowsky and O. Lewis (eds)

Psychotherapies with Children. Washington, DC: American Psychiatric Press.

Bromley, E. (1983) Social class issues in psychotherapy, in D. Pilgrim (ed.) *Psychology and Psychotherapy: Current trends and issues.* London: Routledge and Kegan Paul.

Bromley, E. (1994) Social class and psychotherapy revisited. Paper presented at the British Psychological Society Annual Conference, Psychotherapy Symposium, Brighton, March.

Broverman, K., Broverman, D., Clarkson, F., Rosencrantz, P. and Vogel, S. (1970) Sex role stereotyping and clinical judgement of mental health, *Journal of Consulting and Clinical Psychology*, 34: 1–7.

Brown, G.W. (1996) Onset and course of depressive disorders: summary of a research programme, in C. Mundt, M. Goldstein, K. Hahlweg and P. Fiedler (eds) *Interpersonal Factors in the Origin and Course of Affective Disorders.* London: Gaskell.

Brown, G.W. and Harris, T.O. (1978) *The Social Origins of Depression.* London: Tavistock.

Brown, G.W., Harris, T.O. and Hepworth, C. (1995) Loss, humiliation and entrapment among women developing depression: a patient and non-patient comparison, *Psychological Medicine*, 25: 7–21.

Brown, P. (1995) Naming and framing: the social construction of diagnosis and illness, *Journal of Health and Social Behaviour*, Extra Issue: 34–52.

Browne, D. (1990) *Black People, Mental Health and the Courts.* London: NACRO.

Bruce, M.L., Takeuchi, D.T. and Leaf, P.J. (1991) Poverty and psychiatric status: longitudinal evidence from the New Haven Epidemiological Catchment Area Study, *Archives of General Psychiatry*, 48: 470–4.

Bryer, J.B., Nelson, B.A., Miller, J.B. and Krol, P.A. (1987) Childhood sexual and physical abuse as factors in adult psychiatric illness, *American Journal of Psychiatry*, 144(11): 1426–31.

Bullough, V.L. (1987) The first clinicians, in L. Diamant (ed.) *Male and Female Homosexuality: Psychological Approaches.* New York: Hemisphere.

Burchell, B. (1994) The effects of labour market position, job insecurity, and unemployment on psychological health, in D. Gallie, C. Marsh and C. Vogler (eds) *Social Change and the Experience of Unemployment.* Oxford: Oxford University Press.

Bury, M. (1986) Social constructionism and the development of medical sociology, *Sociology of Health and Illness*, 8: 137–69.

Busfield, J. (1982) Gender and mental illness, *International Journal of Mental Health*, 11(1–2): 44–66.

Busfield, J. (1986) *Managing Madness.* London: Hutchinson.

Buss, A.H. (1966) *Psychopathology.* New York: Wiley.

Carlson, E.A. (1998) A prospective longitudinal study of disorganized/ disoriented attachment, *Child Development*, 69: 1107–28.

Carlson, E.A. and Stroufe, L.A. (1995) Contributions of attachment theory to developmental psychopathology, in D. Cicchetti and D.J. Cohen (eds) *Developmental psychopathology* (Vol. 1). New York: Wiley.

Carmen, E.H., Felip Russo, N. and Baker Miller, J. (1984) Inequality and women's mental health: An overview in P.P. Reiker and E.H. Carment (eds) *The Gender Gap in Psychotherapy: Social Realities and Psychological Processes.* New York: Plenum.

Carpenter, I. and Brockinton, I. (1980) A study of mental illness in Asians, West Indians and Africans living in Manchester, *British Journal of Psychiatry*, 137: 201–5.

Caruso, D.A. (1989) Attachment and exploration in infancy: research and applied issues, *Early Childhood Research Quarterly*, 4: 117–32.

Casement, P. (1985) *On Learning from the Patient.* London: Tavistock.

Celani, D.P. (1993) *The Treatment of the Borderline Patient: Applying Fairbairn's Object Relations Theory in the Clinical Setting.* Madison, CT: International Universities Press.

Celani, D.P. (1997) Perspectives on psychopathology, *Contemporary Psychoanalysis*, 33: 323–33.

Chamberlain, J. (1988) *On our Own.* London: Mind.

Chambless, D.L. and Gillis, M. (1993) Cognitive therapy with anxiety disorders, *Journal of Consulting and Clinical Psychology*, 61: 248–60.

Chapman, A.H. and Chapman, M.C. (1980) *Harry Stack Sullivan's Concepts of Personality Development and Psychiatric Illness.* New York: Bruner/Mazel.

Chen, E., Harrison, G. and Standen, P. (1991) Management of first episode psychotic illness in Afro-Caribbean patients, *British Journal of Psychiatry*, 158: 517–22.

Chessler, C. (1972) *Women and Madness.* New York: Doubleday.

Chodoff, P. and Lyons, H. (1958) Hysteria, the hysterical personality and 'hysterical' conversion, *American Journal of Psychiatry*, 114: 734–40.

Chomsky, N. (1968) *America Power and the New Mandarins.* Harmondsworth: Penguin.

Ciccetti, D., Toth, S.L. and Lynch, M. (1995) Bowlby's dream comes full circle: The application of attachment theory to risk and psychopathology, in T.H. Ollendick and R.J. Prinz (eds) *Advances in Clinical Child Psychology*, Vol. 17. New York: Plenum Press.

Cicchetti, D. (1983) The emergence of developmental psychopathology, *Child Development*, 55: 1–7.

Clare, A. (1976) *Psychiatry in Dissent.* London: Tavistock.

Clarke, D. and Brindley, H. (1993) Black women and HIV: Developing health services to share the challenge, *Clinical Psychology Forum*, 58: 6–9.

Coffer, C.N. and Appley, M. (1964) *Motivation: Theory and Research.* New York: Wiley.

Comer, R.J. (1998) *Abnormal Psychology*, 3rd edn. New York: Freeman.

Cooper, D. (1968) *Psychiatry and Anti-Psychiatry.* London: Tavistock.

Cope, R. (1989) The compulsory detention of Afro-Caribbeans under the Mental Health Act, *New Community*, 15(3): 343–56.

Coppen, A.J. and Doogan, D.P. (1988) Serotonin and its place in the pathogenesis of depression, *Journal of Clinical Psychiatry*, 49: 4–11.

Coulter, J. (1973) *Approaches to Insanity.* New York: Wiley.

Craib, I. (1989) *Psychoanalysis and Social Theory: The Limits of Sociology.* Hemel Hempstead: Harvester Wheatsheaf.

Crits-Christoph, P. (1992) The efficacy of brief psychodynamic psychotherapy: A meta-analysis, *American Journal of Psychiatry*, 149: 151–8.

Crittenden, P.M. (1988) Relationships at risk, in J. Belsky and T. Nezworski (eds) *Clinical Implications of Attachment.* Hillsdale, NJ: Erlbaum.

D'Andrade, R. (1986) Three scientific world views and the covering law model, in D.W. Fiske and R.A. Shweder (eds) *Metatheory in Social Science.* Chicago: Chicago University Press.

Davies, D. (1999) *Insomnia: Your questions answered.* Dorset: Element.

Davies, D.R. (1995) Themes in psychotherapy with the unemployed, *British Psychological Society Psychotherapy Section Newsletter*, 17: 36–46.

Davies, D.R. (1999) Welsh psyche: implications for psychological services, *International Review of Psychiatry*, 11: 197–211.

Day, R.D. and Bahr, S.J. (1986) Income changes following divorce and remarriage, *Journal of Divorce*, 9(3): 75–88.

Dean, G., Walsh, D., Downing, H. and Shelley, P. (1981) First admissions of native born and immigrants to psychiatric hospitals in South East England 1976, *British Journal of Psychiatry*, 139: 506–12.

Department of Health (1998) *Our Healthier Nation.* London: Department of Health.

DeWolff, M.S. and van Ijzendoorn, M.H. (1997) Sensitivity and attachment: A meta-analysis on parental antecedents of infant attachment, *Child Development*, 68: 571–91.

Diamont, L. (1987) *Male and Female Homosexuality: Psychological Approaches.* New York: Hemisphere.

Dilthey, W. (1976) *Selected Writings.* Cambridge: Cambridge University Press.

Dobson, K.S. (1989) A meta-analysis of the efficacy of cognitive therapy for depression, *Journal of Consulting and Clinical Psychology*, 57: 414–19.

Dohrenwend, B. and Dohrenwend, B.S. (1977) Sex differences in mental illness: a reply to Gove and Tudor, *American Journal of Sociology*, 82: 1336–41.

Dozier, M., Stovall, K.C. and Albus, K.E. (1999) Attachment and Psycho-pathology in Adulthood, in J. Cassidy and P.R. Shaver (eds) *Handbook of Attachment: Theory, Research, and Clinical Applications.* London: The Guilford Press.

Dreitzel, H.P. (ed.) (1973) *Childhood and Socialization.* London: Macmillan.

Dunham, H.W. (1957) Methodology of sociological investigations of mental disorders, *Journal of Social Psychiatry*, 3: 7–17.

Dunham, H.W. (1964) Social class and schizophrenia, *American Journal of Orthopsychiatry*, 34: 634–46.

Dutton-Douglas, M.A. and Walker, L.E.A. (1988) *Feminist Psychotherapies: Integration of Therapeutic and Feminist Systems.* Norwood, NJ: Ablex Publishing.

DYG Corporation (1990) *Public Attitudes Toward People with Chronic Mental Illness.* Elmsford, NY: DYG Corporation.

Eichenbaum, L. and Orbach, S. (1982) *Outside In, Inside Out. Women's Psychology: A Feminist Psychoanalytic Approach*. Harmondsworth: Penguin.

Ellenberger, H. (1970) *The Discovery of the Unconscious: The History and Evolution of Dynamic Psychiatry*. New York: Basic.

Elliot, A. (1992) *Social Theory and Psychoanalysis in Transition*. Oxford: Blackwell.

Ellis, A. (1959) Requisite conditions for basic personality change, *Journal of Consulting Psychology*, 23: 538–40.

Ellis, A. (1962) *Reason and Emotion in Psychotherapy*. New York: Stuart.

Erikson, E.H. (1963) *Childhood and Society*, 2nd edn. New York: Norton.

Erinosho, O. and Ayonrinde, A. (1981) Educational background and attitude to mental illness among the Yoruba in Nigeria, *Human Relations*, 34: 1–12.

Evans, M.D., Hollon, S.D., DeRubeis, R.J. et al. (1992) Differential relapse following cognitive therapy and pharmacotherapy for depression, *Archives of General Psychiatry*, 49: 802–8.

Eysenck, H.J. (1955) Psychiatric diagnosis as a psychological and statistical problem, *Psychological Reports*, 1: 3–17.

Eysenck, H.J. (1986) A critique of contemporary classification and diagnosis, in T. Millon and G.L. Klerman (eds) *Contemporary Directions in Psychopathology: Towards the DSM–1V*. New York: Guilford.

Eysenck, H.J. and Wilson, G.D. (1973) *The Experimental Study of Freudian Theories*. London: Methuen.

Fairbairn, W.R.D. (1941) A revised psychopathology of the psychoses and the psychoneuroses, *International Journal of Psycho-Analysis*, 22.

Fairburn, W.R.D. (1952) *An Object-relations Theory of the Personality*. New York: Basic.

Faris, R. and Dunham, H. (1939) *Mental Disorders in Urban Areas*. Chicago: University of Chicago Press.

Feld Institute (1984) *In Pursuit of Wellness: A Survey of California Adults*. Sacramento: California Department of Mental Health.

Fenton, S. and Sadiq, A. (1993) *The Sorrow in My Heart: Sixteen Asian Women Speak about Depression*. London: Commission for Racial Equality.

Fernando, S. (1988) *Race and Culture in Psychiatry*. London: Tavistock.

Fonagy, P. (1999) Psychoanalytic theory from the viewpoint of attachment theory and research, in J. Cassidy and P.R. Shaver (eds) *Handbook of Attachment*. London: The Guilford Press.

Fonagy, P., Steele, M., Steele, H. et al. (1995) Attachment, the reflective self, and borderline states, in S. Goldberg, R. Muir and J. Kerr (eds) *Attachment Theory: Social Developmental, and Clinical Perspectives*. Hillsdale, NJ: Analytic Press.

Forsythe, B. (1990) Mental and social diagnosis and the English Prison Commission 1914–1939, *Social Policy and Administration*, 24 (3): 237–53.

Foucault, M. (1981) *The History of Sexuality*. Harmondsworth: Penguin.

Foulkes, S. H. (1965) Group psychotherapy; the group analytic perspective, in M. Pines and G. Spoem (eds) *Proceedings of the 6th Annual Conference of Psychotherapy*. New York: Karger.

Fowler, D., Garety, P. and Kuipers, E. (1995) *Cognitive Behaviour Therapy for Psychosis: Theory and Practice*. Chichester: Wiley.

Fraiberg, S. (1980) *Clinical Studies in Infant Mental Health: The First Year of Life*. New York: Basic Books.

Freud, A. (1965) *The Writings of Anna Freud: Vol. 6. Normality and Pathology in Childhood: Assessment of Development*. New York: International Universities Press.

Freud, S. (1926) Inhibitions, symptoms and anxiety, in the *Standard Edition of the Complete Psychological Works of Sigmund Freud* (Vol. 20). London: Hogarth Press.

Freud, S. (1930/64) *Civilisation and its Discontents*. London: Hogarth Press.

Freud, S. (1940/1969) *An Outline of Psycho-analysis*. New York: Norton.

Freud, S. (1955) Beyond the pleasure principle, in J. Strachey (ed. and trans.) *The Standard Edition of the Complete Psychological Works of Sigmund Freud* (Vol. 18). London: Hogarth Press. (Original work published in 1920.)

Freud, S. (1957) Five lectures on psycho-analysis, in J. Strachey (ed. and trans.) *The Standard Edition of the Complete Psychological Works of Sigmund Freud* (Vol. 11). London: Hogarth Press. (Original work published 1910.)

Freud, S. (1959) Inhibitions, symptoms, and anxiety, in J. Strachey (ed. and trans.) *The Standard Edition of the Complete Psychological Works of Sigmund Freud* (Vol. 20). London: Hogarth Press. (Original work published 1926.)

Freud, S. and Bleuer, J. (1893/1954) On the psychical mechanism of hysterical phenomena: Preliminary communication, in J. Strachey (ed. and trans.) *The Standard Edition of the Complete Psychological Works of Sigmund Freud* (Vol. 2). London: Hogarth Press.

Fromm, E. (1941) *Escape from Freedom*. New York: Holt, Rinehart and Winston.

Fromm, E. (1942) *Fear of Freedom*. New York: Routledge, Kegan and Paul.

Fryer, D. (1993) Unemployment and mental health. Paper prepared for the British Psychological Society media briefing, *The Psychological Effects of Unemployment*, London, 26 January.

Fryer, D. (1995) Labour market disadvantage, deprivation and mental health, *The Psychologist*, 8(6): 265–72.

Galton, F. (1869) *Hereditary Genius*. London: Macmillan.

George, C., Kaplan, N. and Main, M. (1985) Adult Attachment Interview, 2nd edn. Unpublished manuscript, University of California at Berkeley.

George, C., Kaplan, N. and Main, M. (1996) Adult Attachment Interview, 3rd edn. Unpublished manuscript, University of California at Berkeley.

George, C. and Main, M. (1979) Social interactions of young abused children: Approach, avoidance, and aggression, *Child Development*, 50: 306–18.

Gergen, K. (1985) The social construction movement in modern psychology, *American Psychologist*, 40: 266–75.

Gewirtz, J.L. and Pelaez-Nogueras, M. (1992) B. F. Skinner's legacy to human infant behavior and development, *American Psychologist*, 47: 1411–22.

Gilbert, P. (1992) *Depression: The Evolution of Powerlessness*. Hove: Lawrence Erlbaum.

Goldberg, D. and Huxley, P. (1992) *Mental Illness in the Community*. London: Tavistock.

Goldberg, D. and Morrison, S.L. (1963) Schizophrenia and social class, *British Journal of Psychiatry*, 109: 785–802.

Goldfried, M.R (2000) Consensus in psychotherapy research and practice: Where have all the findings gone? *Psychotherapy Research*, 10: 1–16.

Gottesman, I.I. (1991) *Schizophrenia Genesis: The Origins of Madness*. New York: Freeman.

Gottesman, I.I. and Shields, J. (1972) *Schizophrenia and Genetics: A Twin Study Vantage Point*. New York: Academic Press.

Gove, W.R. (1975) The labelling theory of mental illness: a reply to Scheff, *American Sociological Review*, 40: 242–8.

Gove, W.R. (1984) Gender differences in mental and physical illness: the effects of fixed roles and nurturant roles, *Social Science and Medicine*, 19(2): 77–91.

Greenberg, L.S. and Watson, J. (1998) Experiential therapy of depression: differential effects of client-centred relationship conditions with and without process experiential interventions, *Psychotherapy Research*, 8: 210–24.

Greenwood, J.D. (1994) *Realism, Identity and Emotion: Reclaiming Social Psychology*. London: Sage.

Grof, S. and Bennett, H.Z. (1990) *The Holotropic Mind: The Three Levels of Human Consciousness and How they Shape our Lives*. San Francisco: HarperCollins.

Guidano, G.F. (1987) *Complexity of the Self*. New York: Guilford Press.

Gunnell, D.J., Peters, T.J., Kammerling, R.M. and Borrks, J. (1995) Relation between parasuicide, suicide, psychiatric admissions, and socio-economic deprivation, *British Medical Journal*, 311: 226–30.

Guntrip, H. (1950) *Schizoid Phenomena, Object Relations and the Self*. London: Hogarth Press.

Hall, S. (1988) New Times, *Marxism Today*, October.

Hall, S. (1989) *New Ethnicities. Black Film, Black Cinema*. London: ICA Documents, 27–31.

Hamilton, C.E. (1994) Continuity and discontinuity of attachment from infancy through adolescence. Unpublished doctoral dissertation, University of California at Los Angeles.

Harlow, H.F. (1958) The nature of love, *American Psychologist*, 13: 673.

Harlow, H.F. (1962) The development of affectional patterns in infant monkeys, in B.M. Foss (ed.) *Determinants of Infant Behavior* (Vol. 2). New York: Wiley.

Hartmann, H. (1950) Comments on the psychoanalytic theory of the ego, *Psychoanalytic Study of the Child* (5).

Hartmann, H. (1953) Contribution to the metapsychology of schizophrenia, *Psychoanalytic Study of the Child* (8).

Harvey, D. (1989) *The Condition of Postmodernity*. Oxford: Basil Blackwell.

Hawton, K., Salkovskis, P.M., Kirk, J. and Clark, D.M. (1989) *Cognitive-Behaviour Therapy for Psychiatric Problems: A Practical Guide*. Oxford: Oxford Medical Publications.

Hayley, J. (1963) *Strategies of Psychotherapy*. New York: Grune and Stratton.

Hazan, C. and Shaver, P.R. (1987) Romantic love conceptualized as an attachment process, *Journal of Personality and Social Psychology*, 52: 511–24.

Hazan, C. and Shaver, P.R. (1994) Deeper into attachment theory: Authors' response, *Psychological Inquiry*, 5(1): 68–79.

Heath, G. (1992) Is there therapy after Masson? *Clinical Psychology Forum*, 45: 32–6.

Herman, J.L., Perry, J.C. and van der Kolk, B.A. (1989) Childhood trauma in borderline personality disorder, *American Journal of Psychiatry*, 146(4): 490–5.

Heston, L.L. (1970) The genetics of schizophrenia and schizoid disease, *Science* 167: 249–56.

Heston, L.L. (1992) *Mending Minds: A Guide to the New Psychiatry of Depression, Anxiety, and Other Serious Mental Disorders*. New York: Freeman.

Hitch, P. (1981) Immigration and mental health: local research and social explanations, *New Community*, 9: 256–62.

Hoggett, B. (1990) *Mental Health Law*. London: Sweet and Maxwell.

Holland, R. (1978) *Self and Social Context*. London: Macmillan.

Holland, S. (1992) From social abuse to social action. A neighbourhood psychotherapy and social action project for women, in J.M. Ussher and P. Nicholson (eds) *Gender Issues in Clinical Psychology*. London: Routledge.

Hollender, M. (1971) The hysterical personality, *Contemporary Psychiatry*, 1: 17–24.

Hollingshed, A. and Redlich, R.C. (1958) *Social Class and Mental Illness*. New York: Wiley.

Hollon, S.D. and Beck, A.T. (1994) Cognitive and cognitive-behavioural therapies, in A.E. Bergin and S.L. Garfield (eds) *Handbook of Psychotherapy and Behavior Change*, 4th edn. New York: Wiley.

Horkheimer, M. (1931) Die gegenwartige Lage der Socialphilisophie und die Aufgaben eines Instituts fur sozialforschung, *Frankfurter Universitatstreden*, 37: 13–20.

Horney, K. (1939) *New Ways in Psychoanalysis*. New York: Norton.

Horowitz, A. (1983) *The Social Control of Mental Illness*. New York: Academic Press.

Jacoby, R. (1975) *Social Amnesia: A Critique of Contemporary Psychology from Adler to Laing*. Boston: Beacon Press.

Jahoda, M. (1958) *Current Concepts of Positive Mental Health*. New York: Basic Books.

Jaspers, K. (1959/1997) *General Psychopathology* (trans. J. Hoenig and M.W. Hamilton). Baltimore: Johns Hopkins University Press.

Jones, R. (1991) *Mental Health Act Manual*, 3rd edn. London: Sweet and Maxwell.

Jung, C.G. (1904/7/10) *Studies in Word Association* (The Collected Works of C.G. Jung (CW Vol. 1). Princeton, NJ: Princeton University Press.

Jung, C.G. (1907) *The Psychology of Dementia Praecox*. (CW–3).

Jung, C.G. (1911) *A Criticism of Bleuler's Theory of Schizophrenic Negativism*. (CW–3).

Jung, C.G. (1912/1952) *Symbols of Transformation*. London: Routledge and Kegan Paul.

Jung, C.G. (1913b) The theory of psychoanalysis, *Psychoanalytical Review* 1–40.

Jung, C.G. (1914) *The Content of the Psychosis*. (CW–3).

Jung, C.G. (1916) *The Psychology of the Unconscious*.

Jung, C.G. (1919) *On the Problem of Psychogenesis in Mental Disease*. (CW–3).

Jung, C.G. (1939/47) *Conscious, Unconscious and Individuation*. (CW–9)

Jung, C.G. (1958) *Schizophrenia*. (CW–3).

Karasau, T.B. (1986) The specificity versus non-specific dilemma: Toward identifying therapeutic change agents, *American Journal of Psychiatry*, 183: 687–95.

Karen, R. (1994) *Becoming Attached*. New York: Warner.

Keefe, F.J., Dunsmore, J. and Burnett, R. (1992) Behavioural and cognitive-behavioural approaches to chronic pain. Recent advances and future directions, *Journal of Consulting and Clinical Psychology*, 60: 528–36.

Kelly, G. (1955) *The Psychology of Personal Constructs*. New York: Norton.

Kenny, V. (1985) The post-colonial personality, *Crane Bag*, 9: 70–8.

Kernberg, O.F. (1976) *Object-relations Theory and Clinical Psychoanalysis*. New York: Jason Aronson.

Kestenbaum, R., Farber, E. and Stroufe, L.A. (1989) Individual differences in empathy among preschoolers: Relation to attachment history, in N. Eisenberg (ed.) *New Directions for Child Development: No. 44. Empathy and Related Emotional Responses*. San Francisco: Jossey-Bass.

Kirschenbaum, H. (1979) *On Becoming Carl Rogers*. New York: Delacorte Press.

Klein, M. (1932) *The Psychoanalysis of Children*. London: Hogarth.

Kobak, R. (1999) The emotional dynamics of disruptions in attachment relationships, in J. Cassidy and P.R. Shaver (eds) *Handbook of Attachment; Theory, Research, and Clinical Applications*. London: The Guilford Press.

Kobak, R., Hazan, C. and Ruckdeschel, K. (1994) From symptom to signal: An attachment view of emotion in Marital Therapy, in S. Johnson and L. Greenberg (eds) *Emotions in Marital Therapy*. New York: Brunner/Mazel.

Kohn, M.L. (1973) Social class and schizophrenia, *Schizophrenia Bulletin*, 7: 60–79.

Kohut, H. (1971) *The Analysis of the Self*. New York: International Universities Press.

Korpi, E.R., Kleinman, J.E., Goodman, S.I., et al. (1986) Serotonin and 5-hydroxyindoleacetic acid in brains of suicide victims, *Archives of General Psychiatry*, 43: 594–600.

Kovel, J. (1988) *The Radical Spirit: Essays on Psychoanalysis and Society*. London: Free Association Press.

Kraeplin (1994) *The Diagnostic and Statistical Manual of Mental Disorders*, 4th edn. Washington D.C.: American Psychiatric Association.

Krause, I.B. (1989) Sinking heart: a Punjabi communication of distress, *Social Science and Medicine*, 29(4): 563–7.

Kubie, S. (1954) The fundamental nature of the distinction between normality and neurosis, *Psychoanalytical Quarterly*, 23: 167–204.

Laing, R.D. (1960) *The Divided Self*. London: Tavistock.

Laing, R.D. (1966) *Self and Others*. Harmondsworth: Penguin.

Laing, R.D. (1967) *The Politics of Experience and the Bird of Paradise*. Harmondsworth: Penguin.

Laing, R.D. and Esterson, A. (1964) *Sanity, Madness and the Family*. Harmondsworth: Penguin.

Lambers, E. (1994) Psychosis, in D. Mearns (ed.) *Developing Person-centred Counselling*. London: Sage.

Lampard, R. (1994) An examination of the relationship between marital disillusion and unemployment, in D. Gallie, C. Marsh and C. Vogler (eds) *Social Change and the Experience of Unemployment*. Oxford: Oxford University Press.

Lasch, C. (1978) *The Culture of Narcissism*. New York: Norton.

Lazarus, A.A. (1971) *Behavior Therapy and Beyond*. New York: McGraw-Hill.

Lees, S. (1997) How lay is lay? Chinese students' perceptions of anorexia nervosa in Hong Kong, *Social Science and Medicine*, 44(4): 491–502.

Lieberman, A.F. and Pawl, J.H. (1990) Disorders of attachment and secure base behavior in the second year of life: Conceptual issues and clinical intervention, in M.T. Greenberg, D. Cicchetti and E.M. Cummings (eds) *Attachment in the preschool years: Theory, research, and intervention*. Chicago: University of Chicago Press.

Lieberman, A.F. and Zeanah, C.H. (1995) Disorders of attachment in infancy, *Child and Adolescent Psychiatric Clinics of North America*, 4: 571–687.

Lionell, M. (1989) Reconstruction and character style, *Contemporary Psychoanalysis*, 25: 524–35.

Littlewood, R. and Lipsedge, M. (1982) *Aliens and Alienists*. Harmondsworth: Penguin.

Lomas, P. (1987) *The Limits of Interpretation: What's Wrong with Psychoanalysis?* Harmondsworth: Penguin.

Lorenz, K. (1957) *Instinctive Behavior*. New York: International Universities Press.

Lyons-Ruth, K. (1996) Attachment relationships among children with aggressive behavior problems: The role of disorganized early attachment patterns, *Journal of Consulting and Clinical Psychology*, 64: 64–73.

Mahler, M.S., Pine, F. and Bergman, A. (1975) *The Psychological Birth of the Human Infant*. New York: Basic Books.

Main, M. (1996) Introduction to the special section on attachment and psychopathology: 2. Overview of the field of attachment, *Journal of Consulting and Clinical Psychology*, 54: 237–43.

Main, M. (1997) Attachment: Theory, research, application. Paper presented at the meeting of the American Psychoanalytic Society, New York, December.

Main, M. and Hesse, E. (1990) Parents' unresolved traumatic experiences are related to infant disorganized attachment status: Is frightening and/or frightened parental behavior the linking mechanism?, in M.T. Greenberg, D. Cicchetti and E.M. Cummings (eds) *Attachment in the Preschool Years: Theory, Research and Intervention*. Chicago: University of Chicago Press.

Main, M. and Solomon, J. (1990) Procedures for identifying infants as disorganized/disoriented during the Ainsworth strange situation, in M.T. Greenberg, D. Cicchetti and E.M. Cummings (eds) *Attachment in the Preschool Years: Theory, Research and Intervention*. Chicago: University of Chicago Press.

Malan, D. (1979) *Individual Psychotherapy and the Science of Psychodynamics*. Cambridge: Butterworths.

Marshall, J.R. (1995) Schizophrenia: A constructive analogy or a convenient construct?, in J. Ellwood (ed.) *Psychosis: Understanding and Treatment*. London: Jessica Kingsley.

Marshall, J.R. (1996) Science, 'schizophrenia' and genetics. The creation of myths, *Clinical Psychology Forum*, 95: 5–13.

Maslow, A.H. (1993) *The Farther Reaches of Human Nature*. London: Penguin Arkana.

Masson, J. (1990) *Against Therapy*. London: Fontana.

Masson, J. (1991) *Final Analysis*. London: HarperCollins.

Mayer-Gross, W., Slater, E. and Roth, M. (1954) *Clinical Psychiatry*. London: Cassell.

McCord, J. (1979) Some child-rearing antecedents of criminal behavior in adult men, *Journal of Personality and Social Psychology*, 37: 1477–86.

McGovern, D. and Cope, R. (1987) The compulsory detention of males of different ethnic groups with special reference to offender patients, *British Journal of Psychiatry*, 150: 505–12.

McGovern, D. and Cope, R. (1991) Second generation Afro-Caribbeans and young whites with a first admission diagnosis of schizophrenia, *Social Psychiatry and Psychiatric Epidemiology*, 26: 95–9.

McLeod, J.D. and Kessler (1990) Socioeconomic status differences in vulnerability to understandable life events, *Journal of Health and Social Behavior*, 31: 162–72.

McRae, J.A. and Brody, C.J. (1989) The differential importance of marital experience for the well-being of women and men. A research note, *Social Science Research*, 18(3): 237–48.

Mead, G.H. (1934) *Mind, Self and Society from the Standpoint of a Social Behaviourist*. Chicago: University of Chicago Press.

Miller, P. and Rose, N. (1988) The Tavistock programme: the government of subjectivity and social life, *Sociology*, 22(2): 171–92.

Mills, M. (1992) *SHANTI: A Consumer-based Approach to Planning Mental Health Services for Women*. London: Women's Counselling Services.

Mitchell, J. (1975) *Psychoanalysis and Feminism*. Harmondsworth: Penguin.

Monroe, S.M. and Simons, A.D. (1991) Diathesis-stress theories in the context of life stress research: Implications for the depressive disorders, *Psychological Bulletin*, 110: 406–25.

Mowrer, O. (1947) On the dual nature of learning, *Harvard Educational Review*, 17: 102–48.

Myers, J. (1974) Social class, life events and psychiatric symptoms: a longitudinal study, in B.S. Dohrenwend and B.P. Dohrenwend (eds) *Stressful Life Events: Their Nature and Effects*. New York: Wiley.

Myers, J. (1975) Life events, social integration and psychiatric sympto-matology, *Journal of Health and Social Behaviour*, 16: 121–7.

National Council for One-Parent Families (1987) *Information Sheet*. London: National Council for One-Parent Families.

Nelson-Jones, R. (1982) *The Theory and Practice of Counselling Psychology*. London: Cassell Educational.

Nelson-Jones, R. (1984) *Personal Responsibility Counselling and Therapy: An integrative approach*. London: Harper and Row.

Newnes, C. (1996) The development of clinical psychology and its values, *Clinical Psychology Forum*, 95: 29–34.

Newpin (1992) *Annual Report, 1992*. London: National Newpin.

Nicolson, P. (1989) Counselling women with post-natal depression. Implications from recent qualitative research, *Counselling Psychology Quarterly*, 2(2): 123–32.

Omi, M. and Winant, H. (1987) *Racial Formation in the United States*. London: Routledge.

Ortmeyer, D. (1979) Sexual relatedness in the hysterical character, in L. Saretsky, G.D. Goldman and D. Milman (eds) *Integrating Ego Psychology and Object Relations Theory*. Dubuque, IA: Kendall/Hunt.

Owen, M., Craufurd, D. and St Clair, D. (1990) Localization of a susceptibility locus for schizophrenia on chromosome 5, *British Journal of Psychiatry*, 157: 123–7.

Palmer, R., Christie, M., Cordle, C., Davies, D.R. and Kendrick, J. (1989) *Eating Disorder Questionnaire and Rating Scale* – The CEDRI.

Parker, I., Georgaca, E., Harper, D., McLaughlin, T. and Stowell-Smith, M. (1995) *Deconstructing Psychopathology*. London: Sage.

Parkes, C.M. and Weiss, R. (1983) *Recovery from bereavement*. New York: Basic Books.

Patrick, M., Hobso, R.P., Castle, D., Howard, R. and Maughan, B. (1994) Personality disorder and the mental representation of early social experience, *Development and Psychopathology*, 6: 375–88.

Pavlov, I.P. (1928) *Lectures on Conditioned Reflexes*. New York: Liveright.

Payne, L.R., Bergin, A.E. and Loftus, P.E. (1992) A review of attempts to integrate spiritual and standard psychotherapy techniques, *Journal of Psychotherapy Integration*, 2: 171–92.

Persaud, R. (1998) *Staying Sane: How to make your mind work for you*. London: Metro.

Phillips, D. (1968) Social class and psychological disturbance: the influence of positive and negative events, *Social Psychiatry*, 3: 41–6.

Philo, G., Secker, J., Platt, S. et al (1996) Media images of mental distress in T. Heller et al. (eds) *Mental Health Matters: A Reader*. Basingstoke: Macmillan.

Pianta, R., Egeland, B. and Stroufe, L.A. (1990) Maternal stress in children's development: Predictions of school outcomes and identification of protective factors, in J.E. Rolf, A. Masten, D. Cicchetti, K. Neuchterlein and S. Weintraub (eds) *Risk and Protective Factors in the Development of Psychopathology*. New York: Cambridge University Press.

Pilgrim, D. (1997) *Psychotherapy and Society*. London: Sage.

Pilgrim, D. and Rogers, A. (1994) Something old, something new . . . sociology and the organisation of psychiatry, *Sociology*, 28(2): 521–38.

Pilgrim, D. and Rogers, A. (1997) A confined agenda? Guest editorial, *Journal of Mental Health*, 6(6): 539–42.

Pilgrim, D. and Rogers, A. (1999) *A Sociology of Mental Health and Illness*, 2nd edn. Buckingham: Open University Press.

Pillay, H.M. (1993) The DCP workshop on race and culture issues of equality and power in psychology, *Clinical Psychology Forum*, 61: 24–5.

Poole, R. (1972) *Towards Deep Subjectivity*. London: Allen Lane.

Popper, K.R. (1959) *The Logic of Scientific Discovery*. New York: Basic Books.

Prochaska, J.O. and Norcross, J.C. (1999) *Systems of Psychotherapy: A Transtheoretical analysis*, 4th edn. Monterey, CA: Brooks/Cole.

Purton, C. (1998) Unconditional positive regard and its spiritual implications, in B. Thorne and E. Lambers (eds) *Person-centred Therapy: A European Perspective*. London: Sage.

Ramon, S. (1985) *Psychiatry in Britain: Meaning and Policy*. London: Gower.

Rayner, E. (1993) *The Independent Mind in Psychoanalysis*. London: Free Association Books.

Regier, D., Boyd, J. and Burke, J. (1988) Prevalence of mental disorders in the United States, *Archives of General Psychiatry*, 45: 977–85.

Reich, W. (1933/1975) *The Mass Psychology of Fascism*. London: Pelican.

Reich, W. (1942) *The Function of the Orgasm*. New York: Noonday Press.

Richards, B. (ed.)(1984) *Capitalism and Infancy*. London: Free Association Books.

Richards, B. (1994) *Disciples of Delight: The Psychoanalysis of Popular Culture*. London: Free Association Books.

Richards, B. (1995) Psychotherapy and the injuries of class, *British Psychological Society Psychotherapy Section Newsletter*, 17: 21–35.

Richters, M.M. and Waters, E. (1991) Attachment and socialization: The positive side of social influence, in M. Lewis and S. Feinman (eds) *Social Influences and Socialization in Infancy*. New York: Plenum Press.

Robertson, J. and Bowlby, J. (1952) Responses of young children to separation from their mothers, *Courier of the International Children's Center*, Paris, 2: 131–40.

Robins, L. (1966) *Deviant Children Grow Up*. Baltimore: Williams and Wilkins.

Rogers, C.R. (1957) The necessary and sufficient conditions of therapeutic personality change, *Journal of Consulting Psychology*, 21: 95–103.

Rogers, C.R. (1959) A theory of therapy, personality, and interpersonal relationships as developed in the client-centred framework, in S. Koch (ed.) *Psychology, the Study of a Science, Vol. 3: Formulations of the Person and the Social Context*. New York: McGraw-Hill.

Rogers, C.R. (1961) *On Becoming a Person: A Therapist's View of Psychotherapy*. Boston: Houghton Mifflin.

Rogers, C. R. (1980) *A Way of Being*. Boston: Houghton Mifflin.

Rosenhan, D.L. (1973) On being sane in insane places, *Science*, 179: 250–8.

Rosenhan, D.L. (1975) The contextual nature of psychiatric diagnosis, *Journal of Abnormal Psychology*, 84: 442–52.

Rosewater, L.B. (1985) Schizophrenic, borderline or battered?, in L.B. Rosewater and L.E.A. Walker (eds) *Handbook of Feminist Therapy: Women's Issues in Psychotherapy*. New York: Springer.

Roth, A. and Fonagy, P. (1996) *What Works for Whom? A Critical Review of Psychotherapy Research*. New York: Guilford.

Rothblum, E.M. (1990) Depression among lesbians. An invisible and unresearched phenomenon, *Journal of Gay and Lesbian Psychotherapy*, 1: 67–87.

Rowan, J. (1993) *The Transpersonal: Psychotherapy and Counselling*. London: Routledge.

Rowe, D. (1991) *Breaking the Bonds*. London: Fontana.

Royal College of Psychiatrists (Scottish Division) (1973) *The Future of Psychiatric Services in Scotland*. London: Royal College of Psychiatrists.

Ryle, A. (1990) *Cognitive-Analytical Therapy: Active Participation in Change*. Chichester: Wiley.

Salkovskis, P.M. and Kirk, J. (1997) Obsessive-compulsive disorder, in D.M. Clark and C.G. Fairburn (eds) *Science and Practice of Cognitive Behaviour Therapy*. Oxford: Oxford Medical Publications.

Samelson, F. (1980) J. B. Watson's Little Albert, Cyril Burt's twins, and the need for a critical science, *American Psychologist*, 35: 619–25.

Samuels, A. (1995) *The Political Psyche*. London: Routledge.

Sartre, J.-P. (1963) *Search for a Method*. New York: Knopf.

Sayal, A. (1989) Black women and mental health, *Clinical Psychology Forum*, 22: 3–6.

Schaap, C., Bennun, I., Schinder, L. and Hoogduin, K. (1993) *The Therapeutic Relationship in Behavioural Psychotherapy*. Chichester: Wiley.

Scheff, T. (1966) *Being Mentally Ill: A Sociological Theory*. Chicago: Aldine.

Schutz, A. (1962) *Collected Papers*, Vol. 1. The Hague: Martinus Nijhoff.

Schwartz, H. and Jacobs, J. (1979) *Qualitative Sociology*. New York: Free Press.

Scull, A. (1979) *Museums of Madness*. London: Allen Lane.

Sears, R.R., Maccoby, E. and Levin, H. (1957) *Patterns of Child Rearing*. Evanston, IL: Row, Peterson.

Sedgwick, P. (1982) *Psychopolitics*. London: Pluto Press.

Shaikh, A. (1985) Cross-cultural comparison: psychiatric admission of Asian and indigenous patients in Leicestershire, *International Journal of Social Psychiatry*, 31: 3–11.

Shapriro, M. (1963) A clinical approach to fundamental research with special reference to study of the single patient, in P. Sainsbury and N. Krietman (eds) *Methods in Psychiatric Research*. London: Oxford University Press.

Showalter, E. (1987) *The Female Malady: Women, Madness and English Culture 1830–1980*. London: Virago.

Skinner, B.F. (1990) Can psychology be a science of the mind? *American Psychologist*, 45: 1206–10.

Smail, D. (1987) *Taking Care: An Alternative to Therapy.* London: J.M. Dent and Sons Ltd.

Smail, D. (1993) *The Origin of Unhappiness: A New Understanding of Personal Distress.* London: HarperCollins.

Smail, D. (1996) *How to Survive without Psychotherapy.* London: Constable.

Smart, B. (1990) On the disorder of things: sociology and the end of the social, *Sociology*, 24(3): 397–416.

Smith, H. (1991) Caring for everyone? The implication for women of the changes in community care services, *Feminism and Psychology*, 1(2): 279–92.

Smith, L.J.F. (1989) *Domestic Violence: An Overview of the Literature. A Home Office Research and Planning Report.* London: HMSO.

Soloff, H.P. and Millward, J.W. (1983) Developmental histories of borderline patients, *Comprehensive Psychiatry*, 24: 574–88.

Spence, D. (1982) *Narrative Truth and Historical Truth.* New York: Norton.

Starr, P. (1982) *The Social Transformation of American Medicine.* New York: Basic.

Steele, R.S. (1982) *Freud and Jung: Conflict of Interpretation.* London: Routledge and Kegan Paul.

Stein, L. (1957) 'Social class' gradient in schizophrenia, *British Journal of Preventive and Social Medicine*, 11: 181–95.

Stewart, I. (1989) *Transactional Analysis Counselling in Action.* London: Sage.

Stott, D.H. (1950) *Delinquency and Human Nature.* Dunfermline, Scotland: Carnegie UK Trust.

Stroufe, L.A. (1979) The coherence of individual development, *American Psychologist*, 34: 834–41.

Stroufe, L.A. (1983) Infant-caregiver attachment and patterns of adaptation in preschool: The roots of maladaptation and competence, in M. Perlmutter (ed.) *The Minnesota Symposia on Child Psychology: Vol. 16. Development and Policy Concerning Children with Special Needs.* Hillsdale, NJ: Erlbaum.

Stroufe, L.A. (1990) Pathways to adaptation and maladaptation: Psychopathology as developmental deviation, in D. Cicchetti (ed.) *Rochester Symposium on Developmental Psychopathology: Vol. 1. The emergence of a discipline.* Hillside, NJ: Erlbaum.

Stroufe, L.A. (1996) *Emotional Development.* New York: Cambridge University Press.

Stroufe, L.A. (1997) Psychopathology as development, *Development and Psychopathology*, 9: 251–68.

Stroufe, L.A., Egeland, B. and Kreutzer, T. (1990) The fate of early experience following developmental change: Longitudinal approaches to individual adaptation in childhood, *Child Development*, 61: 1363–73.

Stroufe, L.A. and Fleeson, J. (1986) Attachment and the construction of relationships, in W.W. Hartup and Z. Rubin (eds) *Relationships and Development.* Hillsdale, NJ: Erlbaum.

Sullivan, H.S. (1940) *Conceptions of Modern Psychiatry.* New York: Norton.

Sullivan, H.S. (1953) *Interpersonal Theory of Psychiatry.* New York: W.W. Norton.

Sutherland, S. (1998) *Breakdown: A Personal Crisis and a Medical Dilemma*, 2nd edn. Oxford: Oxford University Press.

Szasz, T.S. (1961a) *The Myth of Mental Illness*. New York: Hoeber.

Szasz, T.S. (1961b) The uses of naming and the origin of the myth of mental illness, *American Psychologist*, 16: 50–65.

Szasz, T.S. (1971) *The Manufacture of Madness*. London: Routledge and Kegan Paul.

Szasz, T.S. (1972) *The Myth of Mental Illness*. London: Routledge.

Szasz, T.S. (1974) *The Second Sin*. London: Routledge and Kegan Paul.

Szasz, T.S. (1992) Crazy talk: thought disorder or psychiatric arrogance?, *British Journal of Medical Psychology*, 65.

Tart, C.T. (1975) *States of Consciousness*. New York: E.P. Dutton and Co., Inc.

Thorndike, E.L. (1898) Animal intelligence: An experimental study of the associative processes in animals, *Psychological Monographs 2* (No. 8).

Thorne, B. (1992) *Carl Rogers*. London: Sage.

Thorne, B. (1994) Developing a spiritual discipline, in D. Mearns (ed.) *Developing Person-centred Counselling*. London: Sage.

Tietze, C., Lemkau, P. and Cooper, M. (1941) Schizophrenia, manic depressive psychosis and socio-economic status, *American Journal of Sociology*, 47: 167–75.

Titmuss, R. (1958) *Essays on the Welfare State*. London: George Allen and Unwin.

Unger, R. (1984) *Passion: An Essay on Personality*. New York: Free Press.

Ussher, J.M. (1991) *Women's Madness: Misogyny or Mental Illness*. London: Harvester Wheatsheaf.

Ussher, J.M. and Nicolson, P. (1992) *Gender Issues in Clinical Psychology*. London: Routledge.

van Ijzendoorn, M.H. (1995) Of the way we are: On temperament, attachment, and the transmission gap: A rejoinder to Fox (1995), *Psychological Bulletin*, 117: 411–15.

Voloshinov, V.N. (1927/1976) *Freudianism: A Marxist Critique*. New York: Academic Press.

von Bertalanffy, L. (1987) General systems theory – a critical review, in Open Systems Group (eds) *Systems Behaviour*. London: Paul Chapman.

Vygotsky, L.S. (1939/1962) *Thought and Language*. Cambridge, MA: MIT Press.

Walker, S. and James, H. (1992) Childhood physical and sexual abuse in women, *Psychiatry in Practice*, 11(1): 15–18.

Warr, P., Jackson, P. and Banks, M. (1988) Unemployment and mental health. Some British studies, *Journal of Social Issues*, 44 (4): 47–68.

Warren, S.L., Huston, L., Egeland, B. and Stroufe, L.A. (1997) Child and adolescent anxiety disorders and early attachment, *Journal of the American Academy of Child and Adolescent Psychiatry*, 36: 637–44.

Waters, E., Merrick, S., Albersheim, L. and Treboux, D. (1995) Attachment security from infancy to early adulthood: A 20-year longitudinal study. Paper presented at the biennial meeting of the Society for Research in Child Development, Indianapolis, March.

Watson, J. B. (1913) Psychology as the behaviourist views it, *Psychological Review*, 20: 158–77.

Watson, J. B. and Rayner, R. (1920) Conditioned emotional reactions, *Journal of Experimental Psychology*, 3: 1–14.

Weiss, R. S. (1975) *Marital Separation: Coping with the End of a Marriage and the Transition to Being Single Again*. New York: Basic Books.

Westermeyer, J. (1985) Psychiatric diagnosis across cultural boundaries, *American Journal of Psychiatry*, 142: 798–805.

Westermeyer, J. and Kroll, J. (1978) Violence and mental illness in a peasant society: characteristics of violent behaviours and 'folk' use of restraints, *British Journal of Psychiatry*, 133: 529–41.

White, J. (2000) Cognitive therapy – what is left when you remove the hype? *Proceedings of the British Psychological Society*, 8: 16.

Wilber, K. (1998) *The Essential Ken Wilber: An Introductory Reader*. Boston: Shambha.

Wilkinson, G. (1975) Patient audience, social status and the social construction of psychiatric disorders, *Journal of Health and Social Behaviour*, 16: 28–38.

Williams, D.R. (1990) Socioeconomic differentials in health: A review and redirection, *Social Psychology Quarterly*, 53: 81–99.

Williams, J.B.W., Gibbon, M., First, M.B. et al. (1992) The Structured Clinical Interview for DSM-111-R (SCID): 2. Multisite test-retest reliability, *Archives of General Psychiatry*, 49: 630–6.

Williams, J., Watson, G., Smith, H., Copperman, J. and Wood, D. (1993) *Purchasing Effective Mental Health Service for Women: A Framework for Action*. Canterbury: University of Kent/MIND Publications.

Winnicott, D.W. (1958) *Collected Works*. London: Hogarth Press.

Winnicott, D.W. (1965) *The Maturational Processes and the Facilitating Environment*. New York: International University Press.

Winnicott, D.W. (1971) *Therapeutic Consultations in Child Psychiatry*. New York: Basic Books.

Wolman, B.B. (1968) *Historical Roots of Contemporary Psychology*. New York: Harper and Row.

Wolpe, J. and Rachman, S. (1960) Psychoanalytic evidence: A critique based on Freud's case of Little Hans, *Journal of Nervous and Mental Disease*, 131: 135–45.

Wootton, B. (1959) *Social Science and Social Pathology*. London: Routledge and Kegan Paul.

World Health Organization (1992) *International Classification of Diseases*, 10th edn. WHO.

Yamamoto, J., James, Q.C. and Palley, N. (1968) Cultural problems in psychiatric therapy, *Archives of General Psychiatry*, 19: 45–9.

Yarrow, M.J., Schwartz, C., Murphy, H. and Deasy, L. (1955) The psychological meaning of mental illness, *Journal of Social Issues*, 11: 12–24.

Yates, A.J. (1970) *Behavior Therapy*. New York: Wiley.

Zadik (1993) Unemployment and mental health. Paper prepared for the British Psychological Society media briefing, *The Psychological Effects of Unemployment*, London, 26 January.

Zanarini, M.C., Gunderson, J.G., Marino, M.F., Schwartz, E.O. and Franken-berg, F.R. (1989) Childhood experiences of borderline patients, *Comprehensive Psychiatry*, 30: 18–25.

Zeig, J.K. (1987) *The Evolution of Psychotherapy*. New York: Brunner/Mazel.

Zigler, E. and Phillips, L. (1961) Psychiatric diagnosis and symptomatology, *Journal of Abnormal Psychology*, 63: 69–75.

Zukav, G. (1979) *The Dancing Wu Li Masters: An Overview of the New Physics*. London: Random House.

Further reading

Andrews, A. and Jewson, N. (1993) Ethnicity and infant deaths: the implications of recent statistical evidence for materialist explanations, *Sociology of Health and Illness*, 15(2): 137–56.

Arlow, J.A. and Brenner, C. (1964) *Psychoanalytic Concepts and the Structural Theory*. New York: International University Press.

Beck, A.T. (1967) *Depression, Causes and Treatment*. Philadelphia: University of Philadelphia Press.

Bowlby, J. (1979) *The Making and Breaking of Affectional Bonds*. London: Tavistock.

Bretherton, I. and Munholland, K. A. (1999) Internal working models in attachment relationships: a construct revisited, in J. Cassidy and P.R. Shaver (eds) *Handbook of Attachment: Theory, Research, and Clinical Applications*. London: The Guilford Press.

Brown, G.W., Harris, T.O. and Bifulco, A. (1986) Long term effects of early loss of parent, in M. Rutter, C. Izard and P. Read (eds) *Depression in Childhood: Developmental Perspectives*. New York: Guilford Press.

Brown, R.M., Strathdee, G., Christie, B.J.R. and Robinson, P.H. (1988) A comparison of referrals to primary care and hospital out-patient clinics, *British Journal of Psychiatry*, 153: 168–73.

CRE (1992) *Race Relations Code: For the Elimination of Racial Discrimination and the Promotion of Equal Opportunity in the Provision of Mental Health Services*. London: Commission for Racial Equality.

Currer, C. (1986) Concepts of mental well- and ill-being: the case of Pathan mothers in Britain, in C. Currer and M. Stacey (eds) *Concepts of Health, Illness and Disease*. Leamington Spa: Berg.

EOC (1992) *Some Facts about Women, 1992*. Manchester: Equal Opportunities Commission.

Fisher, S. and Greenberg, R.P. (1996) *Freud Scientifically Reappraised: Testing the Theories and Therapy*. New York: Wiley.

Frank, L.R. (1990) Electroshock. Death, brain damage, memory loss and brainwashing, *Journal of Mind and Behaviour*, 11: 489–512.

Freud, S. (1914) On Narcissism: an introduction, in the *Standard Edition* (Vol. XIV). London: Hogarth Press.

Freud, S. (1916) Mourning and melancholia, in the *Standard Edition of the Complete Psychological Works of Sigmund Freud* (Vol. XVI). London: Hogarth Press.

Freud, S. (1923/1961) The ego and the id, in the *Standard Edition of the Complete Psychological Works of Sigmund Freud* (Vol. XIX). London: Hogarth Press.

Freud, S. (1940) An outline of psychoanalysis, in the *Standard Edition of the Complete Psychological Works of Sigmund Freud* (Vol. XXIII). London: Hogarth Press.

Freud, S. (1961) The ego and the id, in J. Strachey (ed. and trans.) *The Standard Edition of the Complete Psychological Works of Sigmund Freud* (Vol. 19). London: Hogarth Press. (Original work published 1923.)

Freud, S. (1964) An outline of psycho-analysis, in J. Strachey (ed. and trans.) *The Standard Edition of the Complete Psychological Works of Sigmund Freud* (Vol. 23). London: Hogarth Press. (Original work published 1940.)

Grossman, K.E., Grossman, K. and Schwan, A. (1986) Capturing the wider view of attachment: A reanalysis of Ainsworth's Strange Situation, in C.E. Izard and P.B. Read (eds) *Measuring Emotions in Infants and Children*. New York: Cambridge University Press.

Jung, C.G. (1913a) *Four papers on Psychological Typology*. (CW-6).

Jung, C.G. (1933) *Modern Man in Search of a Soul*.

Jung, C.G. (1939) *On the Psychogenesis of Schizophrenia*. (CW-3)

Jung, C.G. (1956) *Recent Thoughts on Schizophrenia*. (CW-3).

Jung, C.G. (1956) *Two Essays on Analytical Psychology*. New York: Meridian.

Jung, C.G. (1964) *Man and his Symbols*. London: Aldus Books Limited.

Jung, C.G. (1965) *Memories, Dreams, Reflections*. New York: Random House.

Jung, C.G. (1979) *The Collected Works of C.G. Jung*. (25 Vols). London: Routledge and Kegan Paul.

Lionell, M. (1989) Reconstruction and character style, *Contemporary Psychoanalysis*, 25: 524–5.

Main, M. and Goldwyn, R. (1984) Predicting rejection of her infant from mother's representation of her own experience: Implications for the abused-abusing intergenerational cycle, *International Journal of Child Abuse and Neglect*, 8: 203–17.

Main, M. and Solomon, J. (1986) Discovery of a new, insecure disorganized/disoriented attachment pattern, in T.B. Brazelton and M. Yogman (eds) *Affective Development in Infancy*. Norwood, NJ: Ablex.

O'Sullivan, G. and Marks, I. (1991) Follow-up studies of behavioural treatment of phobic and obsessive compulsive neuroses, *Psychiatric Annuals*, 21: 368–73.

Pahl, R.E. (1993) Does class analysis without class theory have a promising future? A reply to Goldthorpe and Marshall, *Sociology*, 27(2): 253–8.

Palmer, S. and Ellis, A. (1993) In the counsellor's chair: Stephen Palmer interviews Dr. Albert Ellis, *Counselling*, 4: 171–4.

Pilgrim, D. (1994) Some are more equal than others. Paper presented at the British Psychological Society Annual Conference, Psychotherapy Symposium, Brighton, April.

Pilgrim, D. and Treacher, A. (1992) *Clinical Psychology Observed*. London: Tavistock/Routlege.

Rice, L.N. (1998) Integration and the client-centred relationship, *Journal of Integrative and Eclective Psychotherapy*, 7: 291–302.

Robertson, J. and Robertson, J. (1989) *Separations and the Very Young*. London: Free Association Books.

Sarason, I.G. and Sarason, B.R. (1981) Teaching cognitive and social skills to high school students, *Journal of Consulting and Clinical Psychology*, 49: 908–19.

Spitz, R. (1958) Discussion of Dr. Bowlby's paper, *Psychoanalytic Study of the Child*, 15: 85–94.

Stroufe, L.A. and Waters, E. (1977) Attachment as an organizational construct, *Child Development*, 48: 1184–99.

Watters, C. (1996) Representations of Asians' mental health in psychiatry, in C. Samson and N. South (eds) *The Social Construction of Social Policy*. London: Macmillan.

Index

CONSCIOUS AND UNCONSCIOUS

David Edwards and Michael Jacobs

All forms of psychotherapy deal with the limitations of our awareness. We have limited knowledge of our creative potential, of the details of our own behaviour, of what motivates us, or of the many factors within and around us which influence the decisions we make and the ways we act. Some therapists, especially those influenced by Freud and Jung, speak of the 'unconscious', giving the unintended impression that it is a kind of realm or domain of activity. Others, reacting against the specifics of Freudian theory, shun the word 'unconscious' altogether. However, so limited is the reach of everyday awareness and such is the range of unconscious factors, that one way or another these limitations must somehow be spoken about, sometimes in metaphor, sometimes more explicitly. This book offers a broad survey of psychotherapy discourses, including the psychoanalytical, the interpersonal, the experiential, the cognitive-behavioural and the transpersonal, and explores a wide range of concepts including repressed instincts, dissociated selves, automaticity, tacit knowledge, unformulated experience, preontological concealment and interactive fields.

Conscious and Unconscious is invaluable reading for advanced students of counselling and psychotherapy and experienced therapists.

Contents
Introduction – Constructing and deconstructing the unconscious – Conscious and unconscious in historical perspective – Freud, Jung and Alder – The development of alternative discourses: Harry Stack Sullivan, Fritz Perls and Medard Boss – Evolving psychoanalytic discourses of the unconscious – Conscious and unconscious in cognitive therapy and science – Invisible worlds, unconscious fields and the nonegoic core: evolving discourses of the transpersonal unconscious – Conscious and unconscious: integrative models and perspectives.

128pp   0 335 20949 1 (Paperback)   0 335 20950 5 (Hardback)